The Public Sector Management Handbook

by

Sandra Nutley and Stephen P. Osborne

Published by Longman Information and Reference,
Longman Group Limited, 6th Floor,
Westgate House, The High, Harlow, Essex CM20 1YR
Telephone: Harlow (0279) 442601; Fax: Harlow (0279) 444501;
Telex: 81491 Padlog.

© Longman Group Limited 1994

All rights reserved. No part of this publication may be reproduced, stored in a retrieval system, or transmitted in any form or by any means, electronic mechanical, photocopying, recording or otherwise, without the prior permission of the Copyright owner or a licence permitting restricted copying issued by the Copyright Licensing Agency Ltd., 90 Tottenham Court Road, London W1P 9HE.

A catalogue record for this book is available from the British Library

ISBN 0–582–21967–1

Printed in Great Britain by BPC Wheatons Ltd, Exeter

Contents

Introduction 1
  What is the public sector? 1
  Managing in the public sector 2
  The structure of this book 5
  References 7
  Guided reading 7

Part 1: The context of public sector management

Chapter 1: Understanding public sector organizations 11
  The changing nature of public sector organizations 11
  Understanding organizational structure 16
  Organizations as systems 24
  Understanding organizational culture 27
  Conclusions 30
  References 30
  Guided reading 31

Chapter 2: The roles and value base of the public sector 32
  Why is there a public sector? 32
  The public–private debate 35
  The wider context of public organizations 37
  The value base of the public sector 37
  Conclusions 39
  Guided reading 40

Part 2: Planning to get it right

Chapter 3: Identifying power and influence 43
  Organizations as coalitions of interest groups 43
  Sources of power 46
  The role of politics in the influencing process 48
  Managing conflict 51
  Using power and influence 54
  Conclusions 54
  References 55
  Guided reading 55

Chapter 4: Working for equality of opportunity and access 57
    Defining equal opportunities 57
    Why is there a need to consider equal opportunities? 58
    Equality of opportunity in employment 60
    Equality of opportunity and access for service users 63
    Improving equality of opportunity 68
    Conclusions 73
    References 73
    Guided reading 74

Chapter 5: Marketing public services 75
    What is marketing? 75
    Characteristics of markets 77
    The components of marketing 78
    Marketing overview 84
    Beyond marketing: business planning 85
    Conclusions 86
    Guided reading 88

Chapter 6: Developing new services 90
    Understanding innovation 90
    Managing the development of new services 95
    Conclusions 100
    References 101
    Guided reading 101

Part 3: Delivering services

Chapter 7: Purchase of service contracting 105
    Introduction 105
    What is a contract? 106
    Important concepts in contracting 108
    Pricing a contract 110
    Contractual relationships 111
    Types of contract 112
    The contracting process 114
    Conclusions 116
    Guided reading 116

Chapter 8: Performance management 118
    Background to performance management 118
    The building blocks of performance management 119
    Performance management 121
    Putting together a performance management system 122
    Performance indicators and value for money 125

At which organizational level should performance be assessed, by whom, and how often?   127
The differing levels of performance management   127
Conclusions   130
References   130
Guided reading   130

Chapter 9: Ensuring quality of service   131
What is quality?   131
Why is quality important?   134
Why evaluate quality?   135
How to measure quality   135
Designing a quality evaluation system   137
Designing your own quality management system   142
Conclusions   144
References   144
Guided reading   145

Chapter 10: Managing finance   146
Managing budgets   147
Estimating costs and planning budgets   155
Costing units of service   159
Conclusions   164
References   165
Guided reading   165

Chapter 11: Making information work for you   166
What is information?   166
What are your information needs?   168
Using information technology   173
Stages in introducing information IT   175
Conclusions   176
References   176
Guided reading   177

Chapter 12: Managing during times of change   178
Understanding the change process   178
Planning and managing change   184
Understanding the effect of change on people   188
Helping people cope with change   189
Conclusions   192
References   192
Guided reading   193

Conclusions: Where next?   195

Acknowledgements

Our thanks go to all those who, over the years, have enabled us to better understand the task of managing in the public sector. In particular, we would like to thank our colleagues at Aston and St Andrews universities for their insight and support. A special debt of gratitude is due to all those students who have studied for a Master's degree in Public Sector Management at Aston University. They have provided a constant source of information, inspiration and interrogation. We are grateful to the following people for reading and commenting on earlier drafts of various of the chapters: Valerie Fournier, Stuart McPhillips, Fiona Wilson and Marian Osborne. Their comments were extremely useful, but the errors and flaws which remain are our responsibility. Finally, Jane Winder and Jean Elkington provided invaluable support in producing the typescript for several of the chapters.

Sandra Nutley

Stephen Osborne.

Introduction

This book is the product of many years of working in and with public sector organizations. Both authors joined public sector organizations in the 1970s and have witnessed the changes which have taken place in these organizations since then. One of the effects of these changes has been the increasing number of demands placed on public sector managers. Many of these managers feel ill-equipped to deal with the new demands of their managerial roles. They come to these roles having first trained and worked in one of the many professions involved with public service delivery. Whilst their professional training may have touched upon some management issues, the main aim then was to develop competent practitioners, not managers. As managers they need additional knowledge and skills for their new roles. The purpose of this book is to help readers to start the process of developing this knowledge and the accompanying skills. It does this by getting you, the reader, to work through a series of exercises which apply the various managerial concepts, ideas and approaches to your own organization, and by encouraging you to think critically about the way that your organization is managed.

What is the public sector?

So far we have used the term 'public sector' several times without defining what we mean by it and hence whom this book is addressed to.

What do you understand by the term 'public sector'? Which organizations do you consider to be a part of the public sector? Make a list of public sector organizations and note down what they appear to have in common.

Your list may have included some of the following:

- *Central government* departments, agencies and services — such as defence, education, health (including the NHS), social security.
- *Local government* departments and services — such as education, social services, housing.
- *Nationalized industries* — such as British Rail, the Post Office.

You may also have noted that increasingly voluntary organizations are taking on the provision of public services on behalf of central and local government.

A common defining feature of public sector bodies in Britain is that their specific powers are derived from Parliament, to whom, in turn, they are ultimately responsible. Many, but not all, public sector organizations are financed mainly via some form of taxation. However, public sector boundaries are becoming increasingly blurred as many private and voluntary sector organizations work as partners or contractors in the delivery of public services.

This book is primarily aimed at those working in the service-based, non-profit oriented parts of the public sector, and hence excludes the nationalized industries. Although voluntary organizations are not formally part of the public sector (as they are not ultimately accountable to Parliament), because of their non-profit making goals, the task of managing in voluntary sector organizations is in many respects similar to managing in public sector organizations. Managers working in voluntary organizations, particularly those concerned with service delivery, are likely to find much of this book equally applicable to their needs.

Managing in the public sector

The blurring of the boundaries between the public and the private sectors might be used as a reason for arguing that the task of management in both sectors is basically the same. Often, however, what is meant by this is that it is reasonable to import private sector management approaches into the public sector. Many of those working in the public sector have expressed concern about such an assumption. Vinten (1992) suggests six items or areas which might distinguish the public sector from the private sector and hence influence the nature of managerial practice:

- *Greater scale, complexity, society-wide basis of most public sector organizations* — The average company is small with a limited product range. Public sector organizations, by contrast, are a major employer of labour. They also tend to take on a wide range of responsibilities which even the multinationals would have difficulty in matching. Moreover, public sector organizations have limited choices about what they do; they often cannot choose to opt out of providing a service.
- *Consistency and conformity more significant in the public sector* — Consistency is important from the service users' point of view. However, this tends to mean that public sector organizations are more governed by the rule book than those in the private sector. There is less scope for individual creativity and initiative.
- *The political element more significant for public sector organizations* — The role of elected members in most public sector organizations is different from the role of board members (although some recent changes, such as the creation of health authority boards have brought them more in line). Given that the political make-up of some local authorities, for example, can change every year, there are likely to be shorter time horizons on the part of policy makers and possibly greater instability in policy direction.
- *The immeasurability of certain public sector work* — It is much easier to measure tangible products than it is to measure the output of social services.
- *Greater accountability to a wider range of audiences in the public sector* — There are a wide range of interest groups to whom public sector organizations need to give an account of their activities. These include: other public sector organizations, taxpayers, service users, suppliers, and financiers (such as banks). Public sector organizations are also required to provide a wider range of information and disclose more about their activities than their private sector

counterparts. It should be noted, however, that there is concern that some of the new forms of organization in the public sector (such as central government agencies and NHS trust hospitals) may be weakening public sector accountability.

- *Hierarchical, bureaucratic, life-time career structure with inflexible pay and promotion more typically a feature of public sector organizations* — Although many private sector organizations have bureaucratic tendencies (see Chapter 1 for a discussion of what is meant by bureaucracy), this is more typical of the public sector where equity of treatment, open accountability and regularity of service are frequently deemed more important. However, both organizational structures and career structures in the public sector are changing and it would be wrong to overemphasise the difference.

To these we can add:

- *Greater dominance by the professions in the public sector* — Although professionals dominate in many private sector partnerships (such as law and accounting firms), when we compare organizations like the NHS and local authorities with large-scale manufacturing companies, the greater dominance of the professions in the former is evident. For example, the medical profession has over the years had a major impact on the function of the NHS (making it more of a 'sickness' service rather than a 'health service').

Whilst the public sector can learn important lessons from private enterprise (and vice versa), these lessons need to be interpreted in the context of public sector organizations. This book aims to provide one such interpretation, whilst at the same time holding on to a public service value base and recognizing the distinctive problems facing managers in the public sector.

It is appropriate to be critical and sceptical of some of the crude approaches to introducing what Vinten (*ibid.*) refers to as a 'managerial ethos' in the public sector. This ethos is concerned with the introduction of a set of standard management procedures and practices which are deemed to be beneficial to all organizations. The guided reading at the end of this introduction provides you with some references to critiques of such an approach. Whilst bearing in mind such criticisms, the aim of this book is to provide a practical guide to introducing and improving what we see as appropriate forms of managerial practice. This does not mean that we see public sector managers as mere agents who implement local and central government policies in an unquestioning manner. We would argue that public sector organizations are made up of a plurality of interests, some of which have more power than others. The task of management will involve engaging with and representing the interests of such groups as service users, professional and support staff, as well as responding to and seeking to influence the politicians who make policy. There is no one right way of managing, but a careful analysis of the circumstances within which you find yourself may suggest that one course of action will be more successful than another. This book aims to provide you with the tools to analyse such circumstances and make informed decisions.

In order to get the most out of this book you should first of all be clear about your own learning needs.

Think about your present job: what managerial tasks does it involve? Now think about any additional managerial tasks and roles which might be required of you in the short to medium term — either because of a development in your present job or due to your changing jobs. Assess the extent to which you feel equipped to deal with each of the tasks you have listed above by using the three point scale of:

— *Good*
— *Adequate*
— *Needs improvement*

We cannot anticipate all the tasks that you may have listed in response to the above exercise. What we do know from research into the nature of managerial work is that the task of managing is richly varied. It is common to identify four main management functions:

— Planning
— Organizing
— Leading
— Controlling

These functions require three key areas of skill:

— Technical skills — expertise within specialist areas such as medicine, law, policing, teaching, finance and computer science
— Human relations skills — the ability to get things done through people
— Conceptual skills — the ability to visualize how things fit together and the direction in which the organization should be moving. That is, being able to 'see the wood despite the trees'.

The extent to which the four main functions of management and the three key skills areas are important in your present job will depend on the level and nature of that role. For example, the requirement to take an overview and use conceptual skills tends to increase as managers become more senior. The need to employ the technical skills of your original professional training tends to decrease as managers become more senior, although new technical skills such as financial, computer and performance management skills will be required.

Our main concern is to help you to develop the technical and conceptual skills we consider important for managing at first line and middle management levels in the public sector. The reason for not focusing explicitly on human relations skills (and hence not including chapters on areas such as motivation, team working and staff selection) is *not* that these skills are considered unimportant, but that they are generic management skills which do not need to be specifically considered within a book on public sector management. The guided reading section at the end of this introduction provides references to the general management texts which deal with these skills adequately. However, this book does not ignore human factors; a key concern throughout the book is to consider the effects of managerial practice on people, how to influence others and where possible take them with you.

The structure of this book

This book endeavours to get you to concentrate on those areas of specific concern to managers in the public sector. It does this by way of three main parts.

The first part is concerned with *the context of public sector management*. Understanding this context is fundamental for developing conceptual skills and an important backdrop for developing appropriate technical skills. Chapter 1 focuses on understanding the nature of public sector organizations. It does this by firstly considering the changes which have occurred in these organizations over the last decade. It then seeks to enable readers to describe and analyse their own organizations by using the concepts of structure, systems and culture. Chapter 2 makes the reader ask some fundamental questions about why we have a public sector and the alternative ways in which its role can be defined. The choice between these alternatives is ultimately a political decision, but whatever choices are made it is argued that two fundamental core values should be honoured: respecting individual freedom and ensuring equality of opportunity. Again the aim of the chapter is to develop conceptual knowledge and sharpen conceptual thinking.

The second part of the book, on *planning to get it right*, is concerned broadly with the planning function of management. The key questions are: where is your organization now, where should it be in the future, and how is it going to get there? The argument of this group of chapters is that you need to analyse and plan if you are to get it right. Plans are doomed to failure if they ignore the distribution of power and influence within an organization, and so this is the subject of the first chapter in this part (Chapter 3). If the core value of equality of opportunity is to be maintained and used to underpin all managerial practice then this needs to be directly considered at an early stage; this is the purpose of Chapter 4. One of the ways in which the public sector has begun to learn from private sector practice is in the use of marketing and business planning. Chapter 5 explores what is meant by these approaches and how they can be applied to good effect in public sector organizations. The final chapter in this part (Chapter 6) acknowledges that in a changing world of needs and demands, good analysis and planning is likely to reveal weaknesses in present services and the need for new services. Chapter 6 considers what we mean by a *new* service and the process of developing and introducing new services.

The final part of the book broadly focuses on *the delivery of services*. In doing so it emphasizes the organizing and controlling functions of management. Again the chapters in this part should lead to the development of both conceptual and technical skills. As Chapter 1 points out, there is an increasing separation of the purchasing from the providing role in public sector organizations, with the corresponding need to establish contractual relationships between purchasers and providers. Chapter 7 considers the practical implications of this by taking readers through the processes and choices involved in purchase of service contracting. All managers in the public sector are having to grapple with the issues of measuring, demonstrating and managing performance. A framework for understanding and managing performance issues is the subject of Chapter 8. As Chapter 1 also highlights, one of the present buzz words in public sector management is quality. Chapter 9 explores what we mean by quality and how public sector managers can seek to ensure quality in the delivery of public services. Many first line and middle managers are now also responsible for managing the finances necessary to the delivery of services. The knowledge and skills they need to do this are introduced in Chapter 10. Information is the life-blood of management and the effective management of information is the subject of Chapter 11. The final chapter in this part, Chapter 12, in many ways summarizes the key issue to have emerged from all preceding chapters — how to manage change and how to manage during times of change. It addresses this issue by asking readers to consider the process of change, the extent to which it can be planned and managed, and, most important of all, how to help people cope with the effects of change.

In order to get the most out of this book you should be clear about your own learning needs. You should also take the time to work though the exercises interspersed throughout the chapters. Only by applying ideas will you develop your understanding and appreciate the strengths and weaknesses of different managerial approaches. The book also encourages you to discuss the ideas you are considering with your peers and others in your organization. This will also be an important part of the learning process. You may find that the book is useful for guiding group study as well as individual endeavour.

Return to the exercise earlier in this introduction which asked you to itemize the knowledge and skills required for your present (and possible future) job. You were also asked to assess your present performance in relation to these knowledge and skill areas. Review this again in the light of what we have subsequently said about the content of this book. Now write down what learning you can reasonably expect, and would like to achieve, by the end of this book. Check out whether your expectations are realistic by matching them against the section at the beginning of each chapter which states 'By the end of this chapter you should. . . .'

Not all your learning needs will be covered by this book. How are you going to address those which are not? The guided reading which follows may help you identify a possible route. Even where a subject is covered in this book, it is unlikely to provide all the answers to your learning needs. For this reason there is a section at the end of each chapter which provides a guide for further reading. Finally, the concluding chapter of the book asks you to consider in more detail where you go from here.

References

VINTEN, G. (1992) 'Reviewing the current managerial ethos', in L. WILLCOCKS and J. HARROW (eds.), *Rediscovering Public Services Management*, McGraw Hill.

Guided reading

A good introduction to the concept of management and its application in the public sector is provided by:

WILLCOCKS, L. and HARROW, L. (eds.) (1992) *Rediscovering Public Services Management*, McGraw Hill (particularly the Introduction, pp. xiii–xxxi).

Chapter 1 by Vinten in the same book is also worth reading.

A more detailed critique of the introduction of managerialism is provided in:

POLLIT, C. (1993) *Managerialism and the Public Services*, Blackwell.

He argues that 'managerialism is a set of beliefs and practices, at the core of which burns the seldom tested assumption that better management will prove an effective solvent for a wide range of economic and social ills' (p. 1).

If you wish to develop your human relations skills, then a good starting point would be:

TORRINGTON, D., and WEIGHTMAN, J. (1994) *Effective Management: People and Organisation*, Prentice-Hall.

Many managers in the public sector have found that 'The Effective Manager' course provided by the Open Business School (part of the Open University) has helped them with many aspects of their management of people. It may be worth finding out whether your organization can give you access to this course or whether the course booklets are available at your local library.

Part 1: *The context of public sector management*

Chapter One:

Understanding public sector organizations

The introduction to this book considered what we mean by the public sector and, in Britain, which organizations are considered to be part of the public sector. A list of organizations in the public sector drawn up in the mid-1970s would look very different from such a list drawn up in the mid-1990s. Even those organizations which appear in both lists are likely to look different. These differences will reflect the nature of their responsibilities, how they are structured to meet those responsibilities, their predominant values, and how they are monitored and held to account. The purpose of this chapter is first of all to consider the ways in which public sector organizations have changed over the last decade and whether these changes 'add up' to a different philosophy of public sector service. The chapter then goes on to consider how to define and analyse the structure of public sector organizations. Next we move on to consider how the various parts of the organization interlock with one another and relate to the world outside of the organization. Finally the chapter acknowledges that by stopping at the dimensions of structures and systems we are likely to miss out important features of the way in which an organization operates. Some of these features are encapsulated within the phrase 'organizational culture', and hence the last part of this chapter considers what we mean by this and how we can analyse an organization's culture.

By the end of this chapter you should:

- be clear about the changing nature of public sector organizations
- be able to describe and analyse your own organization using the concepts of structure, systems and culture

The changing nature of public sector organizations

How has your own organization changed over the last decade? If you are not personally able to comment upon this (because you have not been part of this or a similar organization for long enough), then ask some of your colleagues who have been. In addition to noting down specific changes, try to group these into different types of change.

There should have been no shortage of things to write down in response to the above exercise. You may, however, have had a little more difficulty in trying to group these changes into like categories. Much has now been written about the changes occurring in the public sector during the 1980s. The consensus of opinion is that, taken together, these changes amount to a new philosophy or doctrine as to how public sector services should be provided and managed. This doctrine has been referred to as the 'New Public Management' (for example, by *Public Administration*, Spring 1991). The key elements of the doctrine are listed and discussed below.

The introduction of cash limits and a concern to demonstrate that resources have been well used (value for money)

The use of cash limits as a mechanism for trying to keep public spending in check has become more widespread since the mid-1970s. Although there are still areas, within say the social security budget, where spending is demand-led rather than cash-limited, this is becoming increasingly uncommon. Coupled with this cash-limited cap on spending, is the need to demonstrate that the money allocated has been used well. One way in which value for money has been encouraged and monitored has been via the establishment of a strengthened audit function. In 1982 the Audit Commission was established as the external audit body for local government, and in 1990 it took over responsibility for auditing within the NHS as well. The National Audit Office is the auditing body for central government departments.

Decentralization of service delivery, coupled with devolved responsibility and accountability

In order to keep a tighter control of expenditure there has been a general move in public sector organizations to establish clearer lines of responsibility and accountability. The Financial Management Initiative in central government is one such move in this direction. The consensus of opinion during the 1980s was that those working at the point of delivery are best placed to make decisions on the best use of resources, hence the need to decentralize responsibility out from the centre. The examples are now familiar: local management of schools, decentralization to area offices, the establishment of clinical directorates at sub-hospital level. One of the arguments in favour of decentralization is that those at the point of delivery are in the best position to make decisions regarding budget allocation, and also that their use of resources will be more cautious when they are directly responsible for the budgetary consequences of their actions. It should not be forgotten, however, that some people are suspicious of the underlying reasons for decentralization. The argument runs along the lines that central government is using such decentralization initiatives to weaken the role of local government. Certainly the provision for schools to opt out of local authority control would seem to back the argument that although on the one hand there is decentralization, on the other there is greater centralization.

The identification of explicit standards and measures of performance

An obvious example to illustrate this is the Citizens' Charter launched by John Major in 1991. As a response to the charter initiative public sector services have been establishing the standards that service users should expect and what recourse they have if these standards are not being met. As part of this initiative public sector organizations need to report publicly on their performance on the basis of a standard set of indicators. These indicators should allow the public to make comparisons between different service providers. Some public sector organizations have also established their own standards and performance measures which are not in direct response to external, or at least central government, initiatives. Chapter 8 goes on to consider some of the problems with using performance indicators in making comparisons between service providers. These problems have not prevented their use from becoming more widespread.

An increasing focus on quality and the rights of consumers to have quality public sector services

Throughout the 1980s and into the 1990s quality has become an important buzz word in public sector organizations. Increasingly the concept of quality has been defined from the perspective of service users, rather than merely relying on professional service providers' definition of what constitutes a quality service. The Citizens' Charter, mentioned above, is one of the ways in which the rights of service users to a quality service have been enshrined, although there is some doubt about whether the resulting charters really achieve this aim. Defining quality and ensuring that it exists is not easy. Chapter 9 explores these issues in detail and advises readers on the application of the concept of quality to public sector organizations.

The rights of public service users to have some form of consumer choice

This refers to the trend to allow some users of public sector services to vote with their feet. Hence parents have some rights in relation to the choice of schools for their children, it is now easier for patients to change their general practitioner, and council house tenants can collectively vote not to have the local authority as their landlord any longer. It is questionable just how much practical choice this gives to service users. Also it may be easier for some users to exercise their choices; there are disparities in terms of: (a) the availability of information to users, (b) their ability to use this information and (c) the level of mobility which affects the ability to take up the choices on offer.

Separating out the responsibility for policy setting from that of service delivery

Decentralization of service delivery has led to a questioning of the role of the centre, given that it no longer manages the day-to-day delivery of services. Initially the centre's role was defined in terms of setting the overall policy direction, whilst the decentralized units were concerned with delivery. The establishment of executive agencies (such as the Benefits Agency) in central government was a natural extension of splitting the roles of policy setting and service delivery. The central Department of Social Security is responsible for policy, whilst the Benefits Agency's role is to deliver this policy in the form of benefits and services. The separation of policy formation from service delivery can have consequences for users of services. Service users may feel that it is more difficult to influence policy; there may appear to be an unbridgeable gap between them and the policy makers. Latterly, the role of the centre has been taken one step further by adding to policy setting the role of service purchasing, which is the next item on our list.

The introduction of internal trading

This has been achieved by separating service purchasers from service providers and establishing a contractual relationship between them. Service purchasers estimate the need and/or demand for a service and establish the extent to which these needs and demands are to be met, and in what form. The split between purchasers and providers can be seen at its starkest in the NHS. Service providers are responsible for actually delivering services to the public. Here there are three main purchasers and three main providers of hospital services:

Purchasers	*Providers*
District health authorities	Directly managed NHS hospitals
GP fundholders	NHS Trust hospitals
Private patients	Private hospitals

The forced establishment of contractual relationships between purchasers and providers in organizations like the NHS has had repercussions elsewhere. Many public sector organizations have set up, or are in the process of setting up, voluntary contractual relationships. For example, many central services (such as personnel, finance and training) now contract to provide these services to their internal users. This has lead to a fair amount of internal trading of services within the public sector, with managers acting as purchasers of some services, but at the same time being providers of others. For example, an accountancy section is likely to be a purchaser of computer services from the computer department, and at the same time act as a provider of financial services to other service departments (including the computer department).

Greater competition

The introduction of greater competition into the public sector can be seen as part of the movement to introduce the disciplines of the market place. The first major move in this direction came in 1980 with the requirement that local authorities must tender competitively for certain roads and building work. This led to the establishment of internal direct labour organizations within local authorities which had to compete for the bulk of their work with the private sector. The number of services which had to tender for work competitively was increased in 1988 (to include, for example, refuse collection, street cleaning and the cleaning of buildings). At the time of writing, professional and central services, such as accountancy, are future candidates for compulsory competitive tendering. Competition has been further encouraged by the split between purchasers and providers. Purchasers are encouraged to consider private and voluntary sector providers, as well as their own in-house teams, and in the NHS, for example, there is also some competition between service purchasers (particularly between district health authorities and GP fundholders).

Appointing visible managers who should be 'free to manage'

A good example of this is found in the NHS. The Griffiths report in 1983 recommended the creation of new general manager posts within the NHS. These managers were to provide 'the responsibility drawn together in one person at different levels of the organization for performance' (NHS Management Inquiry, 1983, p. 11).

A stress on private sector styles of management

The language of private business, such as bottom lines, business planning and return on investment, has increasingly become the language of public sector management. Human resource management policies have also reflected this trend, with fixed term contracts and performance-related pay. There are also instances where structural arrangements have mimicked private sector practice. For example, the NHS and Community Care Act has introduced newly styled Health Authority Boards which are intended to operate along business lines.

Refer to the list of ten key elements of the 'New Public Management'. Do any of these elements conflict with one another? How might this conflict be managed?

Your answer to the above exercise may have included some of the following points:

- the problems of delivering a quality service within tight cash limits;
- the danger that performance measurement focuses on the quantitative aspects of a service and not its quality;
- the problems of ensuring that central policy is put into practice in highly decentralized organizations, or organizations where service delivery is contracted out to a third party;
- greater competition not necessarily leading to greater consumer choice.

There are also concerns that decentralization, internal trading and private sector management styles are weakening public sector accountability and endangering the adherence to a public service ethos and value base (see Chapter 2).

If we look at why the changes encompassed by the New Public Management have come about, it is easy to point to legislation, but there is then a need to explain why these legislative changes came into being. One obvious explanation relates to political ideology. Political commentators talk of the breakdown in the post-Second World War consensus, where there was agreement to rebuild the country on the basis of capital and labour working together, supported by the welfare state. The optimism of the 1950s and 1960s began to fade; the goal of full employment was not reached and public services fell into disrepute. The gap left by the crumbling of the consensus was filled by the 'new right ideology' which emphasized the importance of rolling back the frontiers of the state.

However, to talk in terms of change being brought about by a new political ideology would likewise be simplistic. There were a number of other factors which meant that this political ideology was palatable to a large enough slice of the population for the Conservatives to remain in power throughout the 1980s. These factors include the economic conditions of the mid- to late 1970s specifically: (a) the oil crises of the mid-1970s and the ensuing recession; and b) the need, due to the intervention of the International Monetary Fund, to limit public expenditure and get the Public Sector Borrowing Requirement under control. In addition to the economic changes, a number of social changes were taking place. There has been a move away from the rationing mentality of the 1950s to a more consumerist mentality in the 1990s. Hood (1991) talks of the emergence of a more discerning and more demanding public. Finally another enabling, if not causal factor, was the development in technology at this time. Developments in information technology meant that it was possible, for example, to decentralize services because information could instantly be shared and updated at a number of sites.

It would be inappropriate to imagine that the changes grouped under the heading of the 'New Public Management' are the end of the line.

What changes seem to be on the horizon for your organization? What impact are these changes likely to have on:

— *your job*
— *the users of your service*

We have no crystal ball in which to see the future. It seems likely, however, that many of the aspects of the New Public Management will be with us for some time, although some may be emphasized more than others, depending upon the political complexion of central government.

Let us now turn to some of the key concepts by which we are able to describe and understand the organizations within which we work.

Understanding organizational structure

Spend a few moments thinking about how would you describe the way in which your own organization is structured. Jot down the results of your thoughts.

Frequently the first response to the above question is to begin to draw organizational charts to show the formal position of people within the organization, how they are grouped into departments and what the management structure is. You may then begin to reflect on the way in which people actually work together, and might want to begin to superimpose other diagrams. When we make these distinctions between what ought to happen and what does happen we are talking of the distinction between the formal and the informal organization. The formal organization refers to the intended structure of the organization. This structure will consist of designated groups who are meant to work together. The informal organization relates to the unintended network of interactions. These interactions will occur in or between informal groups which have emerged spontaneously, often in response to the need for social contact.

Staying with the formal organization for the moment, it is possible to encapsulate the nature of the formal structure by considering five dimensions:

1. degree of job specialization and formalization
2. criteria by which units and activities are grouped together
3. degree of formalization of rules and regulations
4. types of integrative mechanisms and lateral linkages
5. extent of centralization of the decision-making structure

These dimensions are based upon the work of Child (1984) and Mintzberg (1983). The first of these relates to the extent to which jobs are specialized and differentiated from one another. Horizontal differentiation refers to the division of a task so that many people are working on different aspects of the task at the same level. Vertical differentiation refers to distinguishing between different levels of responsibility and accountability. An example of two housing departments will help to illustrate this (see Figures 1.1 and 1.2).

Figure 1.1: *Organizational diagram of Housing Department A*

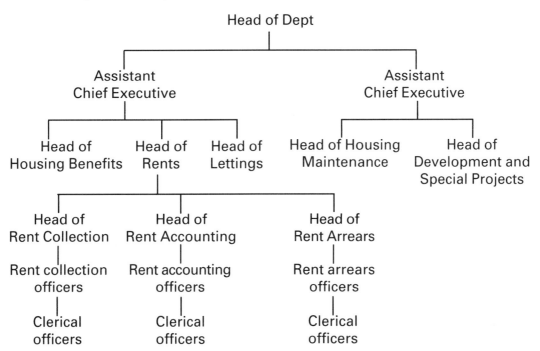

Figure 1.2: *Organizational diagram of Housing Department B*

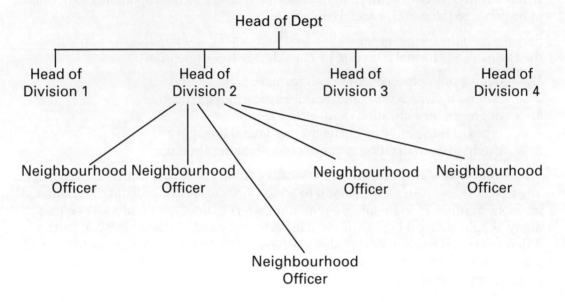

In Housing Department A there is a high degree of job differentiation (both horizontally and vertically). Looking first at horizontal differentiation, there are five main divisions in this department:

— housing benefits
— rents
— lettings
— housing maintenance
— developments and special projects

Each of these divisions is further broken down into a number of specialist tasks. For example the rents division comprises:

— rent collection
— rent accounting
— rent arrears

In this division a rent collection officer does little other than collect rents. Having collected the rents he/she passes them to the rent accounting section who 'balance the books'. Any claims for benefits are dealt with by the housing benefit division. Persistent defaults on rent payment are dealt with by the rent arrears section. None of the officers in the rents division have anything to do with lettings or housing maintenance.

If we consider the level of vertical differentiation in Housing Department A, we find that staff at different levels within the structure have varying levels of responsibility. For example, in the lettings division:

- A clerical worker is able to take details of a lettings enquiry.
- At the next level up, the job of the lettings officer is to maintain the housing waiting list, and he/she is also responsible for allocating points to applicants on the basis of predefined categorization of need; he/she also allocates vacant properties to applicants on the basis of their place on the waiting list.
- The head of the lettings division is responsible for ensuring that policies are adhered to and that all staff within the lettings division liaise with one another.
- The responsibility for revising the lettings policy rests with the assistant chief officer who is responsible for both lettings and rent collection.

By contrast, in Housing Department B there is far less vertical or horizontal differentiation. The department is organized on an neighbourhood basis with the neighbourhood housing officer having a generic role, being responsible for allocating vacant properties, collecting rent and liaising with the housing maintenance officer. Vertical responsibility and accountability is only differentiated into three levels — the chief officer, divisional managers, neighbourhood officers.

The degree of vertical differentiation is often made visible just by looking at the number of levels in the management hierarchy: is it a tall or fairly flat hierarchy? Most large organizations have quite a high degree of differentiation (both horizontally and vertically). The degree of horizontal differentiation may vary over time and in the public sector there seem to be cyclical trends of specialization and generic working. If we take social work as an example, in the 1970s there was a high degree of specialization of social work tasks: mental health, the elderly, mental handicap, hospital social work, children and so on. By the 1980s the trend was for field social workers to act generically, covering all the cases which were referred to them in the locality within which they were based.

From the service users' point of view the degree of horizontal and vertical differentiation is not an academic consideration, but a real issue (although they are unlikely to employ these terms!). Where there is a high degree of horizontal differentiation the users may feel this by the frustration of having to be passed around different people to deal with different aspects of their query or service. Where there is a high degree of vertical differentiation their frustration may be heightened by not being able to find anyone who is able to make a decision on their case.

When discussing horizontal differentiation we referred to working within a locality; this leads us to consider the second dimension of organizational structure, namely how units and activities are grouped together. Once jobs are differentiated there is a need to consider how they are subsequently integrated (or linked). The possibilities include: by function (e.g. physiotherapy, nursing, radiography), by service (e.g. hip replacement), by customer (e.g. the elderly), or by geographical area. Each of these will have implications not only for the way in which the service is managed, but also for how it is experienced by service users.

The third dimension of structure looks at the degree of formalization of rules and regulations, that is, the extent to which there are formal (written down) rules and regulations which employees are expected to follow. In general, public sector organizations have a wide array of rules and regulations covering every aspect of organizational life. These include: rules governing employment practice, rules governing what money can be used for what purposes, and rules governing the treatment of service users. Whilst such rules may often feel like unnecessary red tape, their purpose is to ensure equity of treatment and accountability for the use of public money. The formalization of rules and regulations, together with a high degree of job specialization are two of the features of bureaucracy. The word bureaucracy is often associated with excessive form filling and procedures, but more properly it is a type of organization where formalized rules and job specialization are combined with a hierarchical structure. In public bureaucracies we also expect to find an impersonal attitude in officials; that is, the separation of the office from the individual. People in bureaucracies fulfil roles and they should occupy these roles and be promoted within the organization on the basis of merit. These points are a summary of Weber's (1947) theory of bureaucracy. It is a form of organization which is intended to emphasize precision, speed, clarity, regularity, reliability and efficiency.

The fourth dimension of organizational structure refers to the types of integrative mechanisms and lateral linkages used by the organization. In a simple organizational structure such linkages may be provided solely by managers sitting at the nodal points in the organization's structure. For example, if we refer back to Housing Department A, the managers represented in Figure 1.1 are the main integrating mechanisms: the head of rent collection ensures the necessary liaison between the rent collectors; the head of the rents division ensures liaison between rent collection, rent accounting and rent arrears; the assistant chief housing officer ensures integration between the rents and lettings divisions. However, it is unusual for managers at these nodal points to provide sufficient lateral integration. They are usually supported by management teams at the various levels (e.g. the rents division may have a management team consisting of the heads of rent collection, rent accounting, rent arrears, together with the head of the rents division). Centralized information systems may provide another means of integration. In Chapter 11 we shall look specifically at Management Information Systems. Other lateral linkages could include:

1. a specific post of internal liaison officer
2. temporary project teams which cut across departments and divisions in order to ensure liaison in relation to a specific issue, say, the plight of homeless families
3. permanent project teams which cut across departments and divisions in order to ensure continuing liaison in relation to, say, a particular group of service users

Where organization members feel that there are insufficient or inappropriate formal lateral linkages, informal linkages are often developed.

The final dimension of organizational structure relates to the extent to which decisions are made centrally or whether decision-making powers are devolved. As we said in the section 1, 'The changing nature of public sector organizations' the present trend in the public sector is to try and devolve responsibility for service delivery and operational decision-making to direct service units such as: schools, neighbourhood offices and clinical directorates. Normally responsibility for policy and strategic decisions will remain at the centre.

Now think about the structure of your own organization.

— To what extent are jobs specialized horizontally?
— To what extent are jobs specialized vertically — how many layers are there in the management hierarchy?
— How are jobs grouped together — by function, service, client group or geographical area?
— To what extent are there formalized rules and regulations — to what do these rules and regulations relate?
— What types of integrative mechanisms and lateral linkages exist?
— To what extent is decision-making decentralized?

Now think about the implications:

— What could be done to improve the structure?
— How might changing one of the dimensions affect the others?
— What are the advantages and disadvantages of the proposals you make?
— Where there has already been a structural reorganization, what aims did this have and do they seem to have been achieved?

Writers who have considered organizational structure have combined the five dimensions discussed above and have constructed illustrations (typologies) of common organizational structures. One such typology is provided by Morgan (1987) who distinguishes between:

- *The rigid bureaucracy* — the traditional organizational pyramid under the strict control of the chief executive.
- *The bureaucracy with a senior management team* — the senior management team makes all policy decisions and settles the problems that cannot be handled through the organization's normal routines. Each department head exercises clearly defined authority in relation to his or her area of influence.
- *The bureaucracy with cross-departmental project teams and task forces* — staff at a lower level in the organization are involved in cross-departmental working, but loyalty is still primarily to the department rather than to the project team.
- *The matrix organization* — a feature of this organization is that equal weight is given to functional areas (such as housing, finance, social work) and to geographical areas (north, south) or client groupings (the elderly, under-fives). Thus people working in, say, finance at the same time are members of a geographical team and they frequently work for two 'bosses', their head of function and the head of the geographical or client team.
- *The project organization* — here the organization tackles its core activities through numerous overlapping, autonomous and dynamic project teams. Whilst there may be functional departments these play a supporting role only.

- *The loosely coupled organic network* — this organization operates in a subcontracting mode. It has a small core of staff who set a strategic direction and provide the operational support necessary to sustain the network, but it contracts other individuals and organizations to perform the key operational activities.

Each of these types of organization is illustrated in Figure 1.3. Morgan argues that you can see these six organizations as a continuum denoting a possible evolutionary route. But he argues that evolution beyond model 4 is difficult because of the major change it requires in both culture and politics (both of which are dealt with later in this chapter and in Chapter 3); in fact it denotes more of a revolution than an evolution. The concept of evolution implies that movement in one direction is improvement. Organizations do sometimes move in both directions, and transitions from one form to another are usually messy and disjointed. Model 6 (the loosely coupled organic network) is not necessarily the best type of structure. This will depend upon the situation faced by the organization. Important 'contingent' factors will include the complexity of the task in hand and the extent to which the organization faces changing demands. Matching organization structure to situational demands is known as 'contingency theory'. References to further reading on this can be found in the section on guided reading.

Which of Morgan's types of organization most closely resembles your own organization? What appear to be some of the consequences of this way of organizing?

In the last part of the above exercise you may have listed a number of important consequences. Research on the effects of different types of organizational structure includes the following possible consequences:

- The rigid bureaucracy may well be insensitive to the individual service users' needs, and is likely to be slow in responding to changing needs, but it can be very efficient. Given the key role of the chief executive, he or she will tend to wield substantial power within the organization. People working within the organization may find the only way of getting some things done is to break, or at least bend, some of the rules.
- Highly rule-bound organizations can be a dehumanizing place to work in. The means of doing something can take on greater importance than the ends that are meant to be achieved.
- The bureaucracy with a senior management team is likely to suffer from the same problems as the rigid bureaucracy. The chief executive is unlikely to be so powerful in this organization. Because of the key influence of departmental heads in this structure, the organization may feel like a coalition of 'empires' (with the emperors or empresses being the heads of department) rather than a single organization. However, such a structure may create a corporate organization with corporate goals.
- Introducing project teams and task forces should begin to make the organization somewhat more adaptable and sensitive to service users' needs. There may, however, be a feeling that such task forces have only a temporary

Figure 1.3: *Schematic illustrations of Morgan's six models*

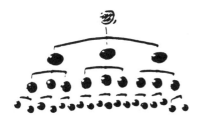

Model 1: The rigid bureaucracy

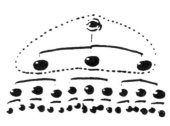

Model 2: The bureaucracy with a senior 'management' team.

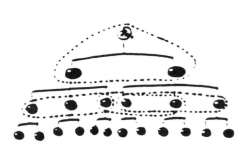

Model 3: The bureaucracy with project teams and task forces

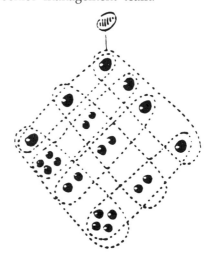

Model 4: The matrix organization

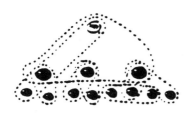

Model 5: The project organization

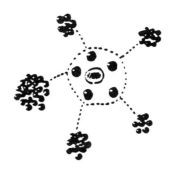

Model 6: The loosely coupled organic network

Source: G. Morgan (1987) *Creative Organization Theory*, Sage, p.66.

impact and that in the medium to long term they make little difference to the functioning of the organization. It can also be quite a difficult form of organization to co-ordinate.
- The matrix organization is likely to be quite a stressful organization within which to work. Individuals working within such a structure may be subject to work overload and role conflict (as a result of working for two bosses). A great deal of time is likely to be spent in meetings. It may have the spin-off advantage that covert conflict is made overt.
- The project organization should feel fluid and dynamic, although this fluidity may lead to individuals experiencing role ambiguity. It should be an exciting if stressful place in which to work, and the changing needs of service users should be addressed.
- The loosely coupled organic network may have a greater sense of strategic direction. How such strategy is translated into practice will be a key to the organization's success, and hence the ability to establish adequate contractual relationships with other parts of the network will be crucial. A concern may be that such an organization may favour in employment terms those groups which are already advantaged in society. The permanent salaried jobs in the core may be predominantly occupied by white middle-class men. Where this core contracts for manual temporary labour, these jobs may be the preserve of disadvantaged groups.

Organizations as systems

Another way of understanding any organization is to begin to look beyond structure in order to consider how the organization operates — that is, its processes and systems. A simple systems view of an organization is to consider it in terms of inputs, organizational processes, outputs and outcomes. We might envisage these elements as being related in the following ways.

Inputs	*Organizational processes*	*Outputs*	*Outcomes*
employees funds service users	→ operating systems administrative systems control system	→ services	→ increased welfare for service users

Inputs refer to the various resources used by an organization — staff, money, materials, and service users. Organizational processes refer to how these various inputs are combined and transformed in the service process. Outputs refer to the services or products produced. Outcomes refer to the effects of these outputs upon the service users or population as a whole. Chapter 9 (on quality) provides a detailed application of systems thinking. For the time being a simple example will suffice; a university, when analysed as a system, might be depicted in the following way:

Inputs
♦ Government money
♦ Other funds

- Buildings and equipment
- Books
- Academic staff
- Non-academic staff
- Students

Processes
- Inputs are organized into departments for the day-to-day operation of the university. Administrative systems vet and administer teaching and research proposals. Control systems audit and hold departments and individuals to account for their performance.

Intermediate outputs
- Lectures
- Seminars
- Laboratory sessions
- Data collection and analysis

Final outputs
- Students with degrees
- Research reports

Outcomes
- Better educated and more able population as a whole

Produce a similar systems analysis of your own organization. Then reflect on the process of doing so. Did you find it easy to make the distinctions between inputs, processes, outputs and outcomes? Does this help to highlight how the organization works to achieve its goals? Does it reveal any potentially redundant processes or intermediate outputs?

Systems analyses which remain at this level of specificity have one main drawback; they are conceived as if they were relatively *closed systems*, that is, as if they were immune from and unaffected by the environment around them. It is normal to draw open systems diagrams of organizations and thus show the main environmental forces impacting upon the organization. Figure 1.4 shows a typical simple open systems diagram. The environmental forces are usually analysed under a number of headings:

— political environment
— economic environment
— social environment
— technological environment

In the case of the university department referred to above the open systems diagram might include the following environmental influences (sometimes referred to by the acronym PEST):

Political
- Policies on funding (e.g. the extent to which universities should be self-funding)
- Policies on access (e.g. the extent to which universities should open up access to mature students)

Figure 1.4: *Illustration of open systems diagram*

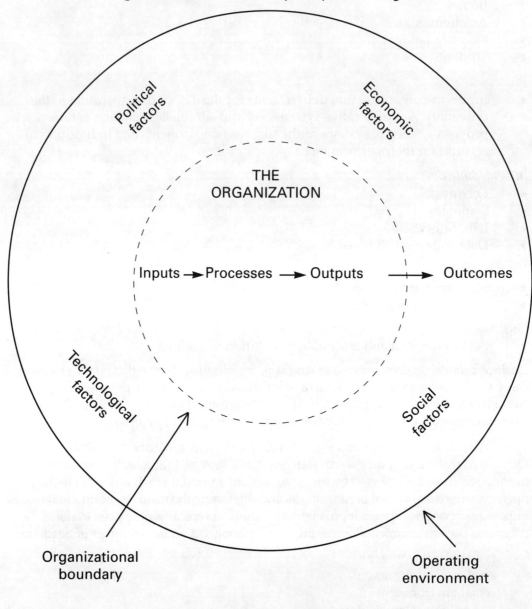

Economic
- State of the economy
- Level of current and planned public expenditure
- Employment level — likely future levels and variations between sectors and localities
- Property and accommodation prices

Social
- Age structure of the population
- Ethnicity of population
- The local community

Technological – Developments in information technology
– Other technological developments

Add to the systems diagram of your own organization the main environmental forces impacting upon it.

Understanding organizational culture

A new architect beginning work in a county council architect's department made the following observations:

> I knew I was entering a different world on the first day. The office looked so regimented with evenly spaced boards and discrete name plates. I felt quite out of place in my shirt and jumper and wished that I had donned the jacket and tie hanging in the wardrobe. There was little in the way of informal conversation about work. Specific design conferences were organized to discuss individual projects rather than people moving freely amongst all members of the office offering comments and advice. My first design conference was an eye opener. After a brief introduction from the lead architect for the project, all members of the group looked to the head of the department to offer his comments first. One by one the rest of the group then reiterated in slightly different words the comments of the head of department. I wanted to say that I didn't agree but knew that this would be frowned upon, I remained silent.

This quotation begins to get at the heart of what we mean by organizational culture.

Before we begin to define the term 'culture' either try to remember your early impressions of the department you now work for. Or if this was too long ago to recall, imagine you are a visitor to the department: what might your first impression be?

The term 'organizational culture' is generally used to refer to all the unwritten values and meanings which abound in organizations. It leads to a code of expectations in terms of how people will behave at work. Harrison (1972) describes organizational culture as: 'the ideologies, beliefs and deep set values which occur in all firms ... and as the prescriptions for the ways in which people should work in these organisations'.

Trying to identify an organizational culture is not necessarily easy. Two alternative ways of trying to assess organizational culture are suggested below.

Firstly, Deal and Kennedy (1982) have suggested an eight-point check list for diagnosing a culture. Organizational culture, they argue, can be discerned by observing the following:

— the physical setting of an organization
— what an organization writes about itself
— how an organization greets incomers

- how staff spend their time, on inward- or outward-focused tasks
- how decisions are made
- how long staff stay in post
- what the content is of internal memoranda and meetings
- what the stories/anecdotes are which staff tell about the organization

An alternative is provided by Robbins (1991) who argues that there appear to be ten characteristics that, when mixed together, arrive at the essence of an organizational culture:

1. Degree of freedom that individuals have to act on their own initiative
2. Degree to which the organization tolerates risk
3. Degree of direction via clear objectives and performance expectations
4. Degree to which co-operation and co-ordinations between departments/units is encouraged
5. Degree of management support for subordinates
6. Degree of control (by rules, regulation and direct supervision)
7. Degree to which employees identify with the organization as a whole
8. Degree to which rewards are based on performance
9. Degree to which employers are encouraged to air conflicts and criticisms openly
10. Degree to which communications are restricted to the formal hierarchy of authority

Each of these characteristics is said to exist on a continuum from low to high. By appraising an organization on these ten characteristics it is possible to obtain a composite picture of an organization's culture.

Which approach to understanding organizational culture makes the most sense to you, Deal and Kennedy's or Robbins's? Depending upon your answer, either:

- *Take the Deal and Kennedy list and write down your observations about your organization for each of their headings. Reflect on your observations and see if it is possible to write a brief summary of how you perceive the culture of your organization.*
- *Draw a line for each of the ten characteristics listed by Robbins. Mark low at one end and high at the other end of each line. Now plot the position of your own organization for each of the ten characteristics. Using these plotted positions, write a short paragraph describing the culture of your organization.*

It is unlikely that everyone in the organization would see its culture exactly in the same way as you have done. It is now popular to distinguish between strong and weak organizational cultures. A strong culture is one which is intensely held and widely shared. A weak culture is the opposite of this. Even where there is deemed to be a strong culture, employees within an organization may still wish to point out that although the culture, overall, is as described, things in their own area of work are rather different. Here the distinction being made is between the dominant culture and other subcultures. A dominant culture refers to the core values that are shared by the majority of an organization's members. A subculture (for, say, a department or a unit) will reflect the dominant core values, but will add other values to these which arise from the unique situation of the particular department or unit.

Consider the picture of the organizational culture which you began to paint in the last exercise. Is this the dominant culture? If so, are there any subcultures you would want to distinguish in addition to the dominant core values? Note that there may not be a dominant culture, but a set of incompatible subcultures with little or nothing in common.

One of the big questions which are asked about organizational culture is how it emerges. Theorists tend to vary according to the extent to which they stress culture emerging as a result of: (a) the complex and largely unplanned development of an organization's history, or (b) a conscious action on the part of senior managers to create such a culture. The former suggests that culture is not something which can be easily created and changed, whilst the latter suggests the opposite. In many private sector firms it is possible to see the important influence of the founder on the subsequent cultural development of the organization (for example, Henry Ford at the Ford Motor Company and Ray Kroc at McDonalds). In many public sector organizations there are no individuals who readily appear to represent the culture of the organization, although Margaret Thatcher's name is sometimes used to describe some elements of public sector culture. In some voluntary organizations, however, the influence of the founder upon the subsequent culture of the organizations may be evident.

Culture is transmitted to employees in a number of ways, including stories, rituals, symbols and language. For example, many women become aware of a macho culture within an organization by a combination of the use of:

- stories — where the hero defied all the organizational odds to get his own way
- ritual — the Friday night drinking session and the Saturday congregation at the rugby or golf club. A great store may also be placed on being the first in and the last out of the office
- language — the male pronoun is always used when referring to senior people in the abstract

If you have not considered it already, think about what stories, rituals, symbols and language abound in your organization. Does this tell you anything additional about your organization's culture?

Many public sector organizations are now trying to develop what they see as an appropriate culture. Such a culture may be encapsulated in slogans such as: *The Caring Council, Where People Come First*. There is a danger, however, that action remains at the level of slogans. The whole thing may be a public relations exercise of image creation with no real substance.

The reasons why organizations try to develop such a shared identity is likely to relate to what are seen as some of the positive aspects of a strong culture:

- it creates a sense of identity
- it sets the boundary of what is appropriate as opposed to inappropriate behaviour
- the existence of shared values can mean the need for less direct supervision and formal controls

However, the research on the link between culture and organizational performance in the private sector does not as yet provide conclusive evidence that there is a strong link.

Strong cultures can, at times, be liabilities. The existence of a strong culture can (as we shall see in Chapter 12) make an organization resistant to change and slow to adapt to changing circumstances. A strong culture may be used as a tool of management control and centralization.

Conclusions

This chapter began by looking at the changing nature of public sector organizations. It then went on to consider how the concepts of structure, systems and culture can be used to understand better the nature of your own organization. The analytical skills you should have developed by working through this chapter are important. Good analytical skills are an important prerequisite for problem spotting and problem solving. A knowledge of the concepts covered in this chapter should enable managers to develop a common framework of understanding, and hence an ability to talk the same language and express their ideas about present organization and future possibilities.

References

CHILD, J. (1984) *Organization: A guide to problems and practice*, Prentice-Hall.

DEAL, T. and KENNEDY, A. (1982) *Corporate Cultures*, Addison-Wesley.

HARRISON, R. (1972) 'How to Describe your Organization', *Harvard Business Review*, Sept-Oct.

HOOD, C.H. (1991) 'A public management for all seasons?', *Public Administration*, **69**, 3–19.

MINTZBERG, H. (1983) *Structure in Fives: Designing Effective Organizations*, Prentice-Hall.

MORGAN, G. (1987) *Creative Organization Theory: A Resourcebook*, Sage.

NHS MANAGEMENT INQUIRY (1983) *Report* ('The Griffiths Report'), Department of Health and Social Security.

ROBBINS, S.P., (1991) *Organizational Behaviour: Concepts, Controversies and Applications*, Prentice-Hall.

WEBER, M. (1947) *The Theory of Social and Economic Organisation*, Oxford University Press.

Guided reading

There are a number of books on public sector management which consider in greater detail the changing context of public sector organizations. Three of these are:

DUNCAN, C. (ed.) (1992) *The Evolution of Public Management: Concepts and Techniques for the 1990s*, Macmillan (especially Part One).

FLYNN, N. (1990) *Public Sector Management*, Harvester Wheatsheaf.

WILLCOCKS, L. and HARROW, J. (eds.) (1992) *Rediscovering Public Services Management*, McGraw-Hill (especially Part One).

If you are interested in the introduction of managerialism into the public sector then read:

POLLITT, C. (1990) *Managerialism and the Public Services*, Blackwell.

A fuller discussion of organizational structure (including contingency theory) can be found in most organizational textbooks. Two recommended texts are:

ROBBINS, S.P. (1991) *Organizational Behaviour: Concepts, Controversies and Applications*, Prentice-Hall.

HUCZYNSKI, A. and BUCHANAN, D. 1991 *Organizational Behaviour*, Prentice-Hall.

A systems approach to organizations is explored in a number of management textbooks. One such book is:

BARTOL, K.M. and MARTIN, D.C. (1991) *Management*, McGraw-Hill (*see* Chapters 2 and 3).

The two organizational behaviour textbooks mentioned above also cover the subject of organizational culture. A further reference worth consulting is:

DEAL, T. and KENNEDY, A. (1982) *Corporate Cultures*, Addison-Wesley.

Chapter Two:
The roles and value base of the public sector

This chapter is intended to make you think about why we have a public sector service and about the role played by the public sector in the UK. By the end of it you should be clear why there is a public sector, and where your agency fits into it. In a perfect free market, with perfect competition and access to information, the market alone would be the most efficient way of deciding what products and services are required in society and at what price. The market, however, is neither free nor perfect, and the public sector consequently has an important role in remedying its deficiencies. By the end of this chapter, you should be clear about:

- market deficiencies and the reasons for the existence of a public sector in the UK;
- the wider societal context in which public sector organizations in general, and yours in particular, operate;

and

- the human values that are represented in the public sector.

Why is there a public sector?

There are three common rationales for the existence of the public sector in market economies such as those in western Europe:

— market failure
— market imperfections
— the 'trust' argument

Market failure

Markets provide services because it is economic to do so — that is, the producer is able to make a profit by selling a good or service. Some goods or services, however, are not economic to produce because the cost of their production leaves little or no margin for profit. Hence the market will 'fail' to produce them. In these cases, therefore, the role of the public sector is either to provide these services itself, because they are deemed to be socially necessary, or to subsidize other suppliers to produce these necessary goods or services.

For much of the post-war period the provision of socially desirable but uneconomic goods and services was deemed to be a core role of the public sector and hence a number of key industries, such as steel, were nationalized. Since the 1970s, however, this view has been challenged, and areas previously thought of as uneconomic for the market, have now been privatized. The most radical proponents of the virtues of the market place argue that most goods/services should be produced within the market place and hence see a very limited role for the state.

One of the important areas where the market fails to provide socially desirable services (and where even the above proponents of the market still see a role for the state) is in the provision of what are referred to as 'public goods'. There are some services which would not be provided by the market because it would not be possible to exclude anyone who chose not to pay for the service. For example, if street lighting is provided in a neighbourhood it is not possible to exclude from enjoying the benefits of the service those individuals who do not pay. This is referred to as the 'free rider' problem. In these cases, there is very little incentive for private producers to provide the good or service because it is not possible to charge each user separately and exclude those who do not pay. Another example of a public good is the armed forces for the defence of the country; once defence cover is provided it is not possible to exclude those who do not wish to pay for it. The response to this problem has generally been for public goods to be provided by governments and paid for by taxation. However, whilst funding via some form of taxation seems necessary, the service does not have to be provided by a public sector organization; the provision of street lighting could be contracted out to a private sector company.

Another defining feature of a public good is that even if it is possible to exclude those who do not pay this may not be desirable as they can be served without any additional cost to the producer. This argument can be used to justify treating museums as a public good. It is possible to exclude those who do not pay, but this would deter those who would benefit from the experience of the museum and who can be served at no additional cost (what is known as 'zero marginal cost' — *see* Chapter 10 on finance for an explanation of marginal costing). Economists refer to this feature of a public good as 'non-rival consumption'; its consumption by one person does not preclude its enjoyment by anyone else. The pleasures of breathing clean air are non-rival. Charging a price which prevents people from breathing clean air unless they have paid for it is undesirable since it could be made available at no additional cost to such people as would benefit from it. Again, the role for the public sector is at least to fund the provision of such public goods, but not necessarily to provide them.

Market imperfections

This is where a market actually exists, but is imperfect in some way. For example, a small number of potential producers or a market which will only support one producer, will lead to monopolistic supply of a good or service and hence limit competition. In such cases, the public sector has a role in either regulating such a monopoly (through the Monopoly Commission), or providing the good/service itself in response to this imperfection. Again, since the 1970s, the latter case is less likely, with the tendency being toward market provision of so-called 'natural monopoly' services such as gas, water, and electricity, rather than provision by the public sector.

A market system should provide both an efficient and an equitable means of allocating resources. Another imperfection of markets, which gets in the way of this, is that potential consumers do not enter the market with equal resources (as in the case of elderly people with differing resources seeking residential care). The role of the public sector in the face of this inequity is to redistribute some of these resources by means of taxation and state benefits.

A third example of the imperfections of the market is that the market acting alone would not consider the social and long-term costs of its activities. For instance, businesses would not take into account the external costs placed on society by their pollution of the environment. The role of the public sector is to regulate these 'external costs' by legislation and environmental health controls.

A final example of the imperfections of the market is that it assumes that when a service or a good is consumed (used), the only person that benefits is the consumer. There are many instances, however, where this is not the case. The people who benefit from a prison service are not necessarily the prisoners or the magistrates who send them there, but society as a whole. It is not only the pupil who benefits from attending school, there are external benefits to society as a whole in having an educated workforce. The argument of external benefits has been used in the past as a rationale for public sector provision of such beneficial services. However, yet again we need to distinguish between public sector funding and service provision, as typified by the discussion about the possible privatization of parts of the police force and the prison service.

The 'trust' argument

There are those who argue that some goods are so sensitive, or their consumers so vulnerable, that their production cannot be left to the market, because of the risk of exploitation. For much of the post-war period, this was the case in regard to the health and social welfare services, though again this position is being challenged by those who assert that more choice and better quality social and health services will only be provided by the market.

A related argument is that the market only works if individuals are the best judges of their own wants and needs. There are many instances where, because of incomplete information, this is not the case. For example, prospective patients are not always in the best position to evaluate different forms of medical treatment and decide which is best for them. The traditional response has been to provide such services publicly rather than jeopardize the well-being of the individual by leaving them to the mercies of the market.

Given the varying rationales for public sector intervention, it is important to consider the roles that your agency performs, as they will affect the management of your service. First, detail the social roles that you think that your organization carries out. Then match them against the list which follows. This is a list of common roles for public agencies. Look through it and tick those that you had already specified when describing the roles of your organization.

Public sector roles

Subsidy to suppliers or public provision of uneconomic goods and services	[ ]
Providing communal (or public) goods	[ ]
Responding to the 'trust' argument by meeting the needs of vulnerable people	[ ]
Responding to market imperfections by:	
Regulating monopolies and mergers	[ ]
Redistributing resources	[ ]
Regulating the external consequences (costs) of market operation	[ ]
Providing externally beneficial goods or services	[ ]
Others (specify)	[ ]

Now consider:

are there any other important roles which have been omitted from the above list?
is it possible to provide a more detailed description of the way in which your organization seeks to fulfil any of these roles and hence the more specific goals it is trying to achieve?
does your agency have different responsibilities to different parts of the community and if so what are the implications of this? (For example, people providing day services for adults with learning disabilities have responsibilities to their actual service users, their carers, and also society in general) and
do any of these roles conflict?

A difficulty that public sector managers often face is that of goal, or role, ambiguity. That is, your agency may be simultaneously trying to achieve quite different goals (such as caring for and controlling behaviourally disturbed teenagers) and/or relating to several different clients (in the above example, the courts, the children and their parents, as well as protecting society in general). This makes managing in the public sector a far more complex task than in commercial organizations, where the main yardstick of success is profit and the balance sheet.

The public–private debate

As will be apparent from what has been said so far, the case for public sector service provision is no longer as self-apparent as it once was, with all of the traditional rationales being challenged. The contention here is that there is still a role for the public sector, albeit one which has different emphases from previous decades. The market continues to need some form of regulation, and the state still maintains a central role in funding, planning and for the most part providing communal (or public) goods and services. The change in emphasis is not so much because the traditional rationales for state intervention have been widely discredited, but more because since 1979 central government has supported an alternative, more limited view of the role of the state. This is important, as it highlights the essential *political* nature of the public sector; it is the political context which shapes public service provision in contemporary Britain.

Your understanding of this should be helped by the diagram in Figure 2.1. This shows how the political framework of the government fundamentally shapes the role that the public sector can have. The vertical dimension represents the economic views of the government, from a belief in the market as the source of funding for publicly needed services, to a belief in the state as the funder. The horizontal dimension represents the social policy views of the government, from a belief in the market as providing necessary public services, to a belief in the role of the state in providing these. This produces four possible different political frameworks for the public sector.

Figure 2.1 *The political context of public services*

ECONOMICAL DIMENSION		SOCIAL DIMENSION
	Market as provider	*State as provider*
Market as funder	Libertarianism ('the new right')	Social market
State as funder	Pluralism	The Welfare State

At the moment we are in the quadrant described as 'pluralism', with public bodies either exhorted or required to be enablers of services, whilst the provision is increasingly coming from the private and voluntary sectors. For most of the post-war period, by contrast, we have operated within the 'welfare state' paradigm with the state as both provider and purchaser of publicly needed services. The other two quadrants are those of 'libertarianism', where the role of the state is a minimalist one, at most administering and enabling the market to plan and provide services; and of the 'social market', with the state providing services, but with finance coming from the private sector (this is not that common in the UK, but the last two Olympic Games are good examples of this at the international level).

It is essential to understand this political context. Many of the decisions about public services (such as who are vulnerable consumers, or what are essential public services) are political ones outside the control of the manager of public services. However, they provide the context and rationale for your agency.

Another way to think about this public–private relationship is by means of the following images:

- *the parallel bars*: this is where the public and private sector provide the same services in competition
- *the extending ladder*: this is where the public sector provides a basic level of services, with the private sector providing 'top-up' services above this basic level

- *the public agent*: this is where the state funds public services, but has no role in their provision, which is carried out by the independent sector.

These images may help you think more clearly about the relationship. It is worth pausing here to consider where your agency fits into this picture. What is its relationship with the private sector and how does it relate to the difficulties of an imperfect market economy?

The wider context of public organizations

In addition to this political context, there are other contextual factors which affect public sector organizations. These include:
- demographic changes (such as the increase in the elderly population of the UK);
- technological changes (the introduction of information technology);
- changes in the perceptions and lifestyle of the population (the impact of 'green issues' upon patterns of personal consumption);

and
- changes in the economic well-being of the country (such as changes in the level of unemployment).

A useful tool in helping you to clarify the contextual factors which are important for your agency is the PEST analysis first mentioned in Chapter 1. PEST stands for:

— **P**olitical factors
— **E**conomic factors
— **S**ocial factors
— **T**echnological factors (this can include both 'hard' technology, such as machinery and 'soft' technology, such as changing skills or organizational processes).

The exercise outlined below is designed to help you think about this wider environment of your organization.

Refer back to Chapter 1, where you considered the main environmental factors impacting upon your organization. Now elaborate on this by systematically going through a PEST analysis for your organization. This should specify the important contextual factors for your organization. Then think about how these factors have changed over the last five years, and may change over the next five years. How have these changes affected your agency and how might they, affect it in the future? Discuss your ideas with your colleagues and see if they agree with you, or have different perceptions. If they see things differently, use this as a basis to discuss your differing perceptions of the context of your agency.

The value base of the public sector

Given the changing context and nature of the public sector, it is important for you to consider if there are any core values which underlie the work of your organization and your own managerial role. Such an 'ethical base', for this is what it is, is important for a number of reasons:

- public officials are often placed in a position of trust by the public (such as for educating their children) and frequently work with the most disadvantaged groups in society (such as profoundly disabled adults), who rely upon them to act in their best interests;
- such officials have an important role in enhancing and supporting fundamental aspects of our society, which are essential to its continued well-being (such as providing essential health care or access to leisure facilities);
- public officials are expected to act in the public interest rather than their own (as for instance in the work of the police force).

and

- given that there is upheaval in the way in which public sector services are both funded and delivered, it is important to establish or reaffirm an underlying set of core values which can serve as a constant benchmark for guiding managerial action.

What do you believe are the core values of your organization? How are these manifested in its work? Is it possible to distinguish between what would be ethical and what would be unethical behaviour?

From the above exercise you may have realized just how hard it can be to specify core values, ethical and unethical behaviour. Notions of what is right or wrong, ethical or unethical are difficult to define and gain agreement on, for it is very much a matter of judgement. Rawls (1971) has argued that there are two principles of social justice, which would form the basis of an ethical code of the public sector:

- everyone has an equal right to the most extensive basic freedom which is compatible with the liberty of others
- socio-economic inequalities and privileges should both be the same for everyone and be ultimately to the advantage of everyone

Rawls is stressing two core values: respecting individual freedom and ensuring equality of opportunity. Seedhouse (1988) includes the following principles as part of the ethical grid he has developed in the context of health care:

— serve needs before wants
— show respect for others and their wishes
— keep promises
— tell the truth
— seek to minimize harm to others
— be able to justify actions by reference to external evidence

Flynn (1990) has suggested a set of ethical values for the management of the public sector. These are:

The right sort of exchange

The management of public services should be built around the relationship between the organization and its users. Recipients of benefits should not be made to feel like criminals, nor should tenants feel that they have no rights. The crucial thing is to agree on the relationship with the users, and to make sure that the service is appropriate to it.

Respect for the task/respect for the producers

An important aspect of the service relationship is the way the organization treats its own workforce. There is still a fund of goodwill in the public sector, which should be harnessed rather than dissipated.

Entitlement

A clear set of customer expectations or entitlements is of as much benefit to the organization as to the users. The Citizens' Charter initiative is a move in this direction.

Accountability

Managerial work in the public sector involves a complicated interface with the political process. Managers need to be clear about their degree of independence and the boundary between politics and management.

User power

In the public sector, users are often powerless in the face of the institution whose services they are using. Organizations have to transfer power to the users to make this relationship more equal.

Freedom and equality

Collective provision need not imply the erosion of individual choice. If choices have to be made collectively, they have to be made through the democratic process. Where possible services should leave scope for individual choice.

There is not space here, nor is it appropriate, to undertake a detailed discussion of the ethics of the public sector. However, it is important that you accept and embrace the need for such an ethical value base for your work. The above brief section should provide you with the base from which to initiate a dialogue on ethics and values with your colleagues and peers.

Conclusions

This chapter has introduced you to the roles and context of the public sector in the contemporary UK, as well as suggesting the need for an ethical value base for it. It has made the point that the roles of public sector organizations are not constant, but can and do change. The direction of this change is heavily influenced by the political context within which public sector organizations operate.

The chapter has asked you to consider the environment of your organization and its particular roles and associated goals. It is important to remember these issues as we examine the 'nuts and bolts' of management in the public sector in subsequent chapters. Management does not occur in a vacuum, but depends upon the above factors for its context and meaning.

References

FLYNN, N. (1990) *Public Sector Management*, Harvester Wheatsheaf.

RAWL, J. (1971) *A Theory of Justice*, Harvard University Press.

SEEDHOUSE, D. (1988) *Ethics*, John Wiley.

Guided Reading

There are two key texts which review the theoretical background to public sector management:

DENHARDT, R. (1993) *Theories of Public Organization*, Wadsworth.

LANE, J. (1993) *The Public Sector*, Sage.

LAWTON, A. (1991) *Organizational Management in the Public Sector*, Longman.

Two other texts look at some of the more practical issues of organizing public and non-profit organizations:

BILLIS, D. (1993) *Organising Public and Voluntary Agencies*, Routledge.

CHALLIS, L. (1991) *Organising Public Social Services*, Longman.

Finally this last text examines some specific managerial issues for the public sector:

WILLCOCKS, L. AND HARROW, I. (ed.) (1992) *Rediscovering Public Services Management*, McGraw-Hill.

Part 2: *Planning to get it right*

Chapter 3:
Identifying power and influence

It is no accident that the topic of power and influence comes first in our section on 'planning to get it right'. This reflects our view that in order to take action, to try new ideas and implement change, the ability to influence others is paramount. This ability to influence others leads us to focus on the concept of power. There are a number of definitions of power and how it manifests itself in organizations. Many definitions start from Dahl's (1957) statement that power is the ability to get another person to do something that he/she would not otherwise have done. The reason why this person would not have done the thing you wanted in the first place relates to the notion of differing interests. Rather than visualizing an organization as a unitary system where everyone is striving towards the same common end with a shared agreement on how to get there, it is important to consider that individuals within an organization will have differing interests in terms of both means and ends. So in this chapter we first of all discuss the identification of these differing interests and then consider how these interests are pursued.

By the end of the chapter you should:

- understand more clearly the concept of power
- be able to identify the main interest groups within your own organization
- be able to describe the differing sources of power used by the interest groups in your organization and those which are available to you
- be clear about what political tactics are used in trying to influence events
- understand how the conflict between varying interest groups might be managed.

Organizations as coalitions of interest groups

Let us consider how we can define and analyse the differing interests present in an organization by first of all starting with your own understanding. How would you define an interest group? What groups of this kind seem to be present in your own organization?

Morgan (1986) defines interests in terms of a complex set of predispositions, embracing goals, values and desires. He goes on to describe interests as relating to three interconnected domains:

- Task — interests relating to the task to be performed
- Career — interests relating to an individual's career

- Outside (or extramural) — interests related to extramural activities

Interests may be pursued on an individual basis or in conjunction with others. Where people join together to pursue common interests, they form interest groups. Such interest groups may form coalitions with other groups to pursue those interests which overlap. Coalitions and interest groups provide an important means of securing desired ends. Coalition building is an important dimension of all organizations, and indeed organizations can be seen overall as coalitions of interests.

A short case study may help to illustrate the above discussion.

> In 1985 a metropolitan district council created a new post as head of community development. This post was directly accountable to the chief executive. Sheila was appointed to this post and she decided that her first task was to analyse the present position of community development. She found that there were three main departments involved in community development initiatives:
>
> — Education
> — Leisure services
> — Social Services
>
> Each of these departments wished to lay claim to community development as their area. Their interest in doing this lay both in the control of resources (or empire building) and in differing conceptions about what community development was about. Leisure Services saw community development as providing facilities and resources for the community; Education thought of it in terms of educating the community; finally Social Services envisaged it in terms of enabling the community to recognize their own interests and further these. Whilst her own views of community development paralleled most closely those of the Social Services Department, she was aware of problems in going down this route. The community development staff that she was to manage had come from the Education Department and were paid on the basis of education grades, which were higher than comparable grades in Leisure or Social Services. Any clear movement away from the Education Department might threaten these workers' career interests, particularly their salary levels. She was also aware that the facilities-based approach to community development was strongly supported by the controlling Labour group and the prominent community leaders, most of whom were also members of the Labour Party. The support for a facilities-based approach seemed to stem from the high visibility of such projects, and thus these individuals could be clearly seen to be doing things for the community. It was also easier to get one-off funding from central government for the development of facilities than it was to get ongoing funding for community development workers.

Consider the above brief case study and list the interests and potential interest groups involved with community development.
Your list may have included the following:

Interest group	Nature of interest
Community development staff	career interest — stay close to Education dept
Labour group } Community leaders }	career interest } — provide facilities for the task interest } community
Sheila	task interest — an enabling approach to community development
Education Department	task interest — an educational approach to community development
Leisure Services Department	task interest — a facilities approach to community development
Social Services Department	task interest — an enabling approach to community development

If we knew more about this particular authority it is likely that we should be able to produce a more detailed analysis of the differing interests involved. For example, it is unlikely that the individuals within the Education department will all share the same views about community development. Maybe one of the education officers has a keen extramural interest in badminton and he or she is only able to promote badminton within the community because of the facilities-based approach to community development. If we were to follow the case study over time we should be able to see how the dynamics of the situation unfold; who sides with whom and what tactics are used in trying to influence the various interest groups.

When we start to think about interest groups we may quickly find that we wish to include groups which are not formally part of the organization. Trying to define what is and what is not part of an organization is becoming increasingly difficult as organizational boundaries begin to blur. There is no problem when all we consider are the full-time paid staff, but we shall soon wish to go beyond this group of people. There will be voluntary staff working with, say, the meals on wheels service. There will be staff contracted and paid to do work on behalf of the organization. There will be businesses which are directly affected by the decisions of a public sector organization, either because they are suppliers of goods or services or because they are regulated by the particular public sector organization (for example, by the enforcement of trading standards). There will be elected politicians, community groups, pressure groups and other representatives (like parent school governors) who are involved with some of the day-to-day business of the organization. There will be the users of public services together with their families and friends. Lastly there will be the general public who may be indirectly effected by some decisions and may well be directly affected by some of the taxation implications.

Now think again about the interest groups in your own organization. You will probably find this more manageable if you focus on that bit of the organization within which you work (e.g. your day centre, ward, neighbourhood office), but by all means look at interests more broadly if you wish. First of all list the core internal interest groups and the nature of their interest. Then consider any important outside groups or those who span the organization's boundary. How strong an interest group are your service users? What constrains their power?

Sources of power

Having identified interest groups we then need to consider how these interests are advanced. If power is the ability to influence people, politics is the means by which this ability is realized. In the next section we shall consider political tactics, but first of all we need to investigate further the concept of power.

What does the term 'power' mean to you? Jot down you initial thoughts.

In considering how the ability to influence others is possible, Handy (1981), drawing upon the work of French and Raven (1960), enumerates five main sources of power:

Source of power	Method of influence
physical (coercive) power	force
resource (reward) power	exchange
position (legitimate) power	rules
expert power	persuasion
personal (referent) power	magnetism

Each of these sources of power is further discussed below:

Physical power relates to the ability to restrain people physically and hence get them to do something they would not otherwise have done. Physical power is not normally manifest in organizations, although the threat of it may be present. In certain public sector services, such as policing, physical power may be an important factor in many aspects of service delivery (e.g. crowd control).

Resource power refers to the control of valued resources. These might be physical, human, financial or information resources. Information refers to 'soft' as well as 'hard' information (the distinction between these two categories is covered in Chapter 11). For resource power to be effective (a) there must be control of the resources, and (b) these resources must be desired by the potential recipient. So the person who controls a budget is likely to have resource power.

Position power is often called legitimate power and it results from the role or position of a person within the organization. It refers to the right to make certain decisions. So team leaders and divisional heads are examples of those likely to have some position power. However, it is seldom sufficient on its own and needs to be ultimately underwritten by the other sources of power, particularly resource power. Handy argues that position power gives the occupant potential control over some invisible assets:

— information
— right of access
— the right to organize

Expert power refers to acknowledged specialist knowledge and skill, usually acquired through professional training outside the organization. Such expertise needs to be recognized for it to be a source of power. The more exclusive this expertise and the more it is seen to be required by the organization, the greater the amount of power which can be exercised. During the 1990s and into the 1990s knowledge of and skills in accounting and computer software engineering have been an important source of expert power within public sector organizations.

Personal power is sometimes referred to as charisma. It relates to a personal ability to persuade others. It depends on personal flair, but may be enhanced by training and development.

Other writers on organizations, such as Robbins (1991), elaborate upon and distinguish between the various categories in this list. Robbins makes the distinction between:

Bases of power — what power-holders control that allows them to manipulate the behaviour of others:

- Coercive power — power that is based on fear
- Reward power — the ability to distribute rewards that others value
- Persuasion power — the ability to allocate and manipulate symbolic rewards
- Knowledge power — the ability to control unique and valuable information

Sources of power — how power-holders come to control the bases of power:

- Position power — influence based on the formal position one holds within the structural hierarchy
- Personal power — influence attributed to one's personal characteristics
- Expert power — influence based on special skills or knowledge
- Opportunity power — influence obtained as a result of being in the right place at the right time.

One of the criticisms of these traditional approaches to power is that they are too individualistic (relating to an individual's power rather than to group power). For example, in the 1960s boom period for public sector building (of houses, schools, and so on) architects and architectural departments wielded considerable expert power. With the drastic cuts in public sector building programmes in the 1980s, this power waned and many local authority architects' departments merged with other departments. Who has power at a particular point in time is affected by a number of situational factors. Hickson *et al.* (1973) identified these situational factors as:

1. Ability to deal with uncertainty
2. Degree of dependence on other units
3. Extent to which activities are substitutable — the power of any part of an

>   organization is lessened if the services it provides can be provided by an alternative source.
> 4. Level of centrality to organization

In an earlier exercise you began to identify the main interest groups in one part of your organization. Now we want you to think about the power of these various interest groups. It may help to think about this first of all in terms of Handy's five sources of power, then go on to consider the situations outlined by Hickson which lead to greater power.

Thus far in this chapter we have been talking about power in terms of the ability of individuals or groups to influence events in the organization. However, there is another side to power. It is not just about being able to influence identifiable decisions overtly. There are many issues which are not openly debated in an organization. Bacharach and Baratz (1970) refer to the importance of non-decisions, that is, the process of agenda setting (the things which are under consideration to be decided on) and the ability to keep things off the agenda. Some theorists (e.g. Lukes, 1974) go further and suggest that in order really to understand power we need to understand why it is that people do not always recognize what their interests are. Stated interests become divorced from real interests by a process of indoctrination, socialization and institutionalization.

The concept of institutionalization is worth exploring, if only briefly. Power relationships and consequent disadvantages become established in the way in which the institutions of our society carry out their day-to-day practice. For example, these routines establish: (a) who has the right to determine an assessment of need; (b) the way in which service users are classified, which may advantage some and disadvantage others; (c) the criteria by which staff are selected to fill varying posts, which may discriminate against certain groups within society. Institutionalization also establishes the accepted roles to be played by different groups in society and their relative power (for example, the accepted and traditional role of women as relatively powerless carers).

The role of politics in the influencing process

Politics is the process by which individuals or interest groups advance their interests. Frequently *politics* is seen as an unsavoury process, but for many theorists politics is healthy and a means of creating order out of diversity. Robbins (1991, p. 407) defines political behaviour as:

> **those activities that are not recognised as part of one's formal role in the organisation, but that influence, or attempt to influence, the distribution of advantages and disadvantages within that organisation.**

Politics is often viewed as a 'zero sum' game, an image which is encouraged by a Machiavellian form of politics (discussed below). The term 'zero sum' is used to denote a finite amount of a resource, say power. So if 'A' backs down on an issue in favour of 'B', 'B' is seen as obtaining a greater share of this finite resource at the expense of 'A'. It is as if power is a cake of predetemined size, and politics is the means by which individuals try to obtain as large a slice as possible. Machiavelli (in *The Prince*, 1513) outlined a number of political tactics which can be used to gain a greater 'slice of the action':

— Alliances
— Lobbying
— Doing favours
— Being present
— Cornering resources
— Being indispensable
— Reciprocal support for a patron
— Being in the right place

These tactics are certainly evident in many organizations, but they are a more overt form of politics than the low-level political activity which may take place on a day-to-day basis.

Robbins (1991) reports on research by Kipnes *et al.* (1984) which considers the use of power tactics. This research identified seven tactical dimensions or strategies used in organizations.

- *Reason* — the use of facts and data to make a logical or rational presentation of ideas
- *Friendliness* — the use of flattery, creation of goodwill, acting humble, and being friendly prior to making a request
- *Coalition* — getting the support of other people in the organization to back up the request
- *Bargaining* — the use of negotiation through the exchange of benefits or favours
- *Assertiveness* — use of a direct and forceful approach such as demanding compliance with requests, repeating reminders, ordering individuals to do what is asked, and pointing out that rules require compliance (NB those familiar with assertiveness training may question whether some of these tactics are more aggressive than assertive)
- *Higher authority* — gaining the support of higher levels in the organization to back up requests
- *Sanctions* — use of organizationally derived rewards and punishments such as preventing or promising a salary increase, threatening to give an unsatisfactory performance evaluation, or withholding a promotion

These tactics are used in different orders of priority depending upon whether managers are trying to influence superiors or subordinates (for further details *see* Robbins, p. 405).

Think of a situation in your own organization where you were aware of a conflict of interests. Which of the above tactics were used by the parties involved and how? Could they have used other tactics?

Robbins (1991) considers which situations or cultures promote politics:

- When an organization's resources are declining or when the pattern of resources is changing
- Cultures characterized by low trust, role ambiguity, unclear performance evaluation systems, zero sum reward allocation practices and democratic decision-making.

Machiavellian politics is frequently seen as covert and manipulative, and this sits uneasily with the values of many of those working in the public sector. Women often see this as a male view of power and politics in organizations and are uncomfortable with it. The problem is that many traditional views of power and politics treat it as if it were truly a zero sum game. That is, there is a finite amount of power and if one person gains more, it has to be at the expense of another. An alternative view is that if one person enables another to do something, say by giving them delegated authority, the power of both may be enhanced and not necessarily at the expense of others. The term 'empowerment' is often used to describe the process of giving power to others. The reader should note, however, that the term 'empowerment' continues to be used in a number of different ways (*see* Osborne, 1994).

The important message for public sector managers at all levels is that they are never without any ability to influence events. This may seem hard to envisage at times, but it is exactly at these times that it is important to weigh up situations and consider the possibilities for you to influence events, either individually or in conjunction with others. The ability to influence events as an individual working alone is probably limited in most cases, and for this reason it is important to avoid isolation and begin networking with others. An exercise which may help you identify your own power and political situation is to draw a 'power net'[1.] Such a net will look something like this:

[1.] This exercise is adapted from Ryan, M. and Fritchie, R. (1982) *Career Life Planning Workshops for Women Managers*, Bristol Polytechnic/Manpower Services Commission.

The people around the edge are those who have an important effect on your work; they may be higher or lower than yourself in the hierarchy, and either inside the organization or outside it (if they are clients or customers for example). The questions to ask yourself are:

1. what sort of power does each person in your 'net' have in relation to you?
2. do they have the right to decide what you do?
3. what information do you need?
4. what is their power based on?
5. what sort of power do you have in relation to them?

You can also think of the power net in terms of dependence:

6. who depends on you for what?
7. who do you depend on, for what?

Information is crucial to your success in influencing others and politically useful information is unlikely to be gained via the formal channels of communication. You need to network with others in order to tune into the informal information which passes around the organization. It is a vital part of understanding organizational politics and hence being able to influence these politics. Why should you wish to influence events? The reason stems from our vision of organizations *not* as unitary organizations, where everyone is pursuing the same common agreed goals, but as pluralist coalitions where people pursue divergent and possibly competing goals. There will be a need to negotiate workable compromises and form coalitions for the delivery of services. But situations change over time and this negotiation is ongoing. Hence there is continually a need to represent your own and selected others interests in the unfolding dynamics of the situation. There is no one right way to organize and provide services. What services should be provided by the public sector is an inherently political, as well as a moral decision. What is rational to one group may be irrational to another, hence the importance of identifying your own interests and those of others who may not be so readily able to represent their own interests. Resistance and opposition to new initiatives should be seen as a normal and healthy feature of a pluralist organization. This naturally leads us to consider the management of change which is the subject of Chapter 12.

Managing conflict

An acceptance that organizations comprise different, divergent and sometimes competing interests implies that conflict is inevitable. An 'interactionist' view of conflict believes not only that conflict is inevitable, but also that it is an essential part of organizational life. Conflict is said to keep the organization dynamic, creative and self-critical. Thomas (1976) has outlined five strategies for managing conflict: avoiding, accommodation, competing, collaborating and compromising. These strategies are plotted in Figure 3.1 according to two dimensions:

Figure 3.1: *Dimensions of conflict-handling orientation*

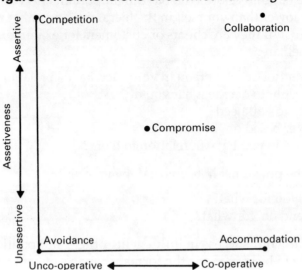

Source: K. W. Thomas, 'Conflict and conflict Management', in M. D. Dunnette (ed.) (1976) *Handbook of Industrial and Organizational Psychology*, Rand McNally, p. 900. Reprinted by permission of John Wiley.

1. how assertive each party is in pursuing their own concerns
2. how co-operative each is in satisfying the concerns of others

Thus *competition* refers to an assertive and unco-operative strategy where one party pursues their own interest regardless of the impact of this on others. Such a strategy is seen as creating a win–lose situation. *Collaboration* is an assertive and co-operative strategy where a problem-solving approach is adopted; confronting differences but trying to search for solutions which will serve all parties. This often referred to as a win–win strategy. *Avoidance* is an unassertive and unco-operative strategy where although a conflict of interests is recognized, one party to this chooses not to pursue their interest. The result is withdrawal from the source of conflict or suppression of the differences. *Accommodation* is an unassertive and co-operative strategy where one party may try to resolve the conflict by putting the interests of the other party above their own. Finally *compromise* is a strategy which falls in the middle of both the assertiveness and co-operativeness dimensions. Here the parties to a conflict trade off some of their interests in order to reach a workable compromise.

Thomas (1977) argues that one conflict-handling style is rarely appropriate for all situations. He has sought to identify the situations in which one style is preferable over another. His conclusions are reproduced in Figure 3.2.

Now think about conflict situations in your own workplace. Does one conflict-handling style seem to be favoured over another? What style do you tend to adopt? Try to think of situations where you have employed each of the style. How far does each of your situations accord with what Thomas considers to be appropriate situations for that particular conflict-handling style? What styles are you happiest/unhappiest with?

Figure 3.2: *Conflict-handling orientations*

When to use the five conflict-handling orientations

Conflict handling orientation		Appropriate situations
Competition	1	When quick, decisive action is vital (e.g. in emergencies)
	2	On important issues where unpopular actions need implementing (e.g. in cost cutting, enforcing unpopular rules, discipline)
	3	On issues vital to organization's welfare when you know you're right
	4	Against people who take advantage of non-competitive behaviour
Collaboration	1	To find an integrative solution when both sets of concerns are too important to be compromised
	2	When your objective is to learn
	3	To merge insights from people with different perspectives
	4	To gain commitment by incorporating concerns into a consensus
	5	To work through feelings that have interfered with a relationship
Avoidance	1	When an issue is trivial, or more important issues are pressing
	2	When you perceive no chance of satisfying your concerns
	3	When potential disruption outweighs the benefits of resolution
	4	To let people cool down and regain perspective
	5	When gathering information supersedes immediate decision
	6	When others can resolve the conflict more effectively
	7	When issues seem tangential or symptomatic of other issues
Accommodation	1	When you find you are wrong — to allow a better position to be heard, to learn, and to show your reasonableness
	2	When issues are more important to others than yourself — to satisfy others and maintain co-operation
	3	To build social credits for later issues
	4	To minimize loss when you are outmatched and losing
	5	When harmony and stability are especially important
	6	To allow subordinates to develop by learning from mistakes
Compromise	1	When goals are important, but not worth the effort or potential disruption of more assertive modes
	2	When opponents with equal power are committed to mutually exclusive goals
	3	To achieve temporary settlements to complex issues
	4	To arrive at expedient solutions under time pressure
	5	As a backup when collaboration or competition is unsuccessful

From K. W. Thomas (1977) 'Towards multidimensional values in teaching: the example of conflict behaviours', *Academy of Management Review,* July, p.487.

Using power and influence

You should now have the building blocks which enable you to identify interest groups, understand power and the process of influencing others, and how the naturally occurring conflict within an organization can be managed. We now want you to think about how you can use this understanding when 'planning to get it right'.

Think of a problematic situation that you are having to manage. For example, it could be a change in work practice that you are having to introduce. Work through the following steps:

1. What interest groups are represented in this situation? Do groups of people share common interests and are they aware of this? Have they formed into interest groups to represent their interests?
2. Draw a 'power net' of the people/groups involved and place yourself at the centre of this net. Who depends on whom for what? What power sources are open to you, what power sources are open to others?
3. What political tactics can be used in influencing others? Are certain tactics to be preferred over others? If so, why?
4. Is there conflict between the people/groups in your 'power net'? If not, do you see conflict as likely to develop? How are you going to handle this conflict? What seems the most appropriate approach given the situation? Does your proposed action give them power or take it away?

Conclusions

This chapter has emphasized that an understanding of power and the ability to influence others is important for all managers, including those in the public sector. Whilst on one level it can be argued that public sector employees administer the policy decisions made by elected politicians, administering a changing policy agenda will require political skills (with a small *p*) in convincing those affected by the changes to adopt new ways of working. In addition such policies usually leave some latitude for local interpretation. Many central policy changes have their origins in local initiatives and experimentation. You will need the political knowledge and skills outlined in this chapter to enable you to experiment with new forms of service delivery and then promote a more extensive adoption of successful experiments.

Later chapters in this book focus on the need for service deliverers to consult with service users in order to identify service needs. Consultation processes are likely to highlight a range of interests and concerns. It will be important for you as an individual, and as a group member, to be able to represent your interests and those of others.

References

BACHARACH, P. and BARATZ, M.S. (1970) *Power and Poverty: Theory and Practice*, Oxford University Press.

DAHL, R.A. (1957) 'The Concept of Power', *Behavioural Science*, 2, quoted in C. HAM and M. HILL (1984) *The Policy Process in the Modern Capitalist State*, Wheatsheaf Books.

FRENCH, J.R.P. and RAVEN, B. (1960) 'The bases of social power' in D. CARTWRIGHT and A.F. ZANDER (eds.) *Group Dynamics*, 2nd edn, Row, Peterson.

HANDY, C.B. (1981) *Understanding Organisations*, Penguin.

HICKSON, D.J., HININGS, C.R., LEE, C.A., SCHNECK, R.E. and PENNINGS, J.M. '"A strategic contingencies" theory of intra-organisational power', *Administrative Science Quarterly*, **16** (2), 216–29.

KIPNES, D., SCHMIDT, S.M., SWAFFIN-SMITH, C. and WILKINSON, I. (1984) 'Pattern of Managerial Influence: Shotgun Managers, Tacticians and Bystanders', *Organisational Dynamics*, Winter, 58–67.

LUKES, S. (1974) *Power: A Radical View*, Macmillan.

MACHIAVELLI, N. (1513) *The Prince*, reprinted by Penguin in 1981.

MORGAN, G. (1986) *Images of Organisation*, Sage.

OSBORNE, S.P. (1994) 'The language of empowerment', *International Journal of Public Sector Management*, forthcoming.

ROBBINS, S.P. (1991) *Organisational Behaviour: Concepts, Controversies and Applications*, Prentice-Hall.

THOMAS, K.W. (1976) 'Conflict and conflict management' in M.D. DUNNETTE (ed.) *Handbook of Industrial and Organizational Psychology*, Rand McNally.

——— (1977) 'Towards multidimensional values in teaching', *Academy of Management Review*, July, p. 487.

Guided reading

A good place to start if you want to read more about the traditional view of power and conflict is to look at one or two of the standard organizational behaviour texts. The two mentioned in this chapter (Robbins, 1991 and Handy, 1981) would be an appropriate place to begin. You may also like to consult Chapter 11 in:

WILSON, D.C. and ROSENFELD, R.H. (1990) *Managing Organisations*, McGraw-Hill.

One of the mainstream writers on power in organizations is Jeffrey Pfeffer. Those wishing to study the subject in more detail may wish to consult:

PFEFFER, J. (1992) *Managing with Power*, Harvard Business School Press.

An extract from this book is reproduced in:

MABEY, C. and MAYON-WHITE, B. (1993) *Managing Change*, Paul Chapman.

Possibly a more thought-provoking analysis of power is provided by Mangham. His book looks at politics and organizational change, and is useful further reading for both this chapter and Chapter 12:

MANGHAM, I. (1979) *The Politics of Organisational Change*, Association Business Press.

An interesting case study of power which also provides an interesting read is:

PETTIGREW, A. (1973) *The Politics of Organizational Decision Making*, Tavistock.

If you want to read more about non-traditional views of power, particularly of the relationship between gender and power, the following would be a good starting point:

KANTER, R.M. (1977) *Men and Women of the Corporation*, Basic Books (particularly Chapter 7).

MARSHALL, J. (1984) *Women Managers: Travellers in a Male World*, Wiley (particularly Chapters 3 and 4).

DICKSON, A. (1982) *A Woman in Your Own Right: Assertiveness and You*, Quartet Books.

HENLEY, N.M. (1977) *Body Politics: Power, Sex and Non-verbal Communication*, Prentice, Hall.

Chapter Four:
Working for equality of opportunity and access

One of the areas where it is advantageous to identify power and influence is in bringing about change to promote greater equality of opportunity. We would argue that working for equal opportunities should be a core concern for all managers. This chapter considers why this should be so and goes on to discuss how equality of opportunity in both employment and service delivery might be addressed. In doing so, the focus is mainly on inequality due to race and gender. Other sources of inequality, such as disability and age, are equally important, but there is insufficient space in this chapter to do justice to them all. By the end of the chapter you should:

- be clearer about what is meant by equality of opportunity
- understand some of the reasons for the existence of inequality
- have considered the position of women and black people within your own organization
- be able to describe what your organization is doing to improve equality of opportunity and whether this is enough
- understand the key steps in improving equal opportunities

Defining equal opportunities

What do you understand by the term equal opportunities? Try to write down a definition of equal opportunities and what it entails.

A Probation Service officer provided the following definition about what we mean by equality of opportunity in the public sector.

> Equality of opportunity is about the elimination of discrimination in our society. It is about the effective use of human resources and positive action measures to ensure employment opportunities and service provision are bias free and made readily available to people from within a target group. Equality of opportunity involves the breakdown and removal of discriminatory structures, biased policies and prejudicial practices in organizations. It seeks to replace processes that perpetuate inequality with better and more effective ways of working which provide equal access for all service and employment opportunities.

As can be seen from this quotation, the public sector has an important role in ensuring equality of opportunity in two areas. Firstly, as an employer the public sector has often taken on the responsibility of trying to provide a good role model in relation to employment practices. Secondly, the public sector has an important role to play in ensuring equality of opportunity and access in service delivery. Most 'public' services should by their very nature be open to all members of the public, regardless of factors such as race, gender, disability, and age.

Why is there a need to consider equal opportunities?

Let us start with your own thoughts. Do you think there is a need for public sector managers to concern themselves with equal opportunities? If yes, why? If not, why not?

If you answered 'yes' to the above question your reasons may have included:

- The need to comply with legislation
- The need from an ethical standpoint to give people an equal opportunity
- The argument that not giving people an equal opportunity can lead to a poor use of resources. For example, many argue that if organizations do not endeavour to accommodate a career break for women whilst they have children, their skills, knowledge and abilities may be permanently lost to the organization. Any earlier investment in the training and development of such women may be squandered. Even if they do return to work in the organization, they may find barriers to their progress and hence their abilities may not be used to their full potential.
- The argument that if organizations and management groups reflect more closely the make-up of society they may be better able to design and provide services appropriate to that society. A diversity of perspectives can be a great asset to an organization.

If you answered 'no' to the question in the above exercise, we find it hard to think of good reasons to support such a view.

- As we discuss below such a view cannot be supported on the grounds that equality of opportunity already exists.
- The argument might be that equal opportunities do not make 'good business sense'. For example, arguments for sex discrimination might use figures which demonstrate that on average women spend fewer years in the labour force than men, have a shorter average length of service and higher average turnover (*see* Rubenstein, 1987). The argument would then run that as an employer invests money in recruitment and training, it makes sense to increase the rate of return on investment by favouring the recruitment of men. There are two problems with such an argument:
    - average figures do not necessarily apply to women as individuals;
    - the so-called 'facts' may be selectively partial.

    On the latter point, a study by Homans (1987) found that pregnancy did not emerge as the largest cause of wastage in the NHS. The group of leavers with the shortest length of service were those who left for promotion or sideways moves. In addition men were more likely than women to be early leavers. Another study (Angle and Perry, 1981) found that women were more committed to their organizations than men. The explanation given is that women enjoy less inter-organizational mobility than men and this restriction may increase commitment.

Let us return to the issue of inequality and the existence of legislation to counter this. We live in an unequal society — people have different opportunities depending upon their race, gender, social class, age, religion, disability, or sexual orientation. Discrimination in relation to gender and race is addressed by legislation (in particular the Sex Discrimination Acts of 1975 and 1986 and the Race Relations Act 1976). This legislation covers both discrimination in employment opportunities and discrimination in relation to a person seeking to use a public facility or service. The legislation applies to both direct and indirect discrimination. The law in Britain defines direct discrimination as treating a person less favourably than another on grounds of sex or race. Indirect discrimination consists of applying a requirement or condition which, although applied equally to all persons, is such that a smaller proportion of women (or of a particular racial group) can comply with it and it cannot be shown to be justified (for example, a rule about clothing or uniforms which disproportionately disadvantages a racial group and cannot be justified on, say, safety grounds).

Despite the existence of legislation in these areas, an analysis of the extent to which the position of women, black and other minority ethnic groups has changed makes depressing reading. Why might this be so? Public sector organizations tend to have a better track record in at least developing policies and strategies to address equal opportunities issues. However, such policies often have only a limited effect because many of the reasons for discrimination in our society are deeply rooted. For example, any consideration of racial discrimination needs to place it within the context of the slave trade and Britain's colonial past. Racism can be said to have arisen from slavery; it was necessary to believe that black people were 'lacking in character', 'intellectually inferior' and dangerous (*see* Fryer, 1989) in order to justify their enslavement. Whilst slavery may have gone, the beliefs prevalent then live on. They may continue to be adhered to in the beliefs and attitudes of some individuals, but more importantly, they have become woven into many of the routine practices of British institutions. Mullard (1991, p. 12) points out that:

> An antiracist approach cannot be developed without accepting that racism is an institutionalised feature of the history and social, economic, political and ideological fabric of British Society.

He goes on to say that:

> What should be teased out here is that the notion of the black individual in history and history in the black individual is a complex process of the re-experiencing of past oppressions through the experiencing of present day oppressions (*ibid.*, p. 13).

It is not unlawful in Britain to discriminate against a person on the grounds of disability, but the 1944 Disabled Persons (Employment) Act established a quota system in relation to the employment of disabled people. It states that every employer of more than twenty people has to employ enough disabled people to make up a quota (currently 3 per cent) of their workforce. If an organization is under quota it should not employ another non-disabled person unless it has obtained a special permit. As might be guessed from the date of the Act, this legislation arose out of the political and moral pressure to make provision for the war disabled. Its effectiveness over time has declined. More and more employers are requesting and receiving special permits to allow them to remain under quota.

Equality of opportunity has been a concern for providers of public services for at least the last two decades, but some would argue that its importance has been heightened by the changes currently occurring in the public sector. We outlined in Chapter 1 those changes which centre around the introduction of the market into the public sector and the establishment of contractual rather than managerial relationships. The relationship between service purchasers and providers becomes defined by a contract, and there are concerns that such contracts will not place sufficient weight on equal opportunity issues. Two booklets by the National Council for Voluntary Organizations (NCVO, 1991, 1993) document some of these concerns. They include:

- Those who specify and evaluate bids for contracts will place more emphasis on efficiency and cost savings, than on effectiveness and equal opportunities.
- Small voluntary organizations, particularly black voluntary organizations, will be marginalized in the contracting process; they will not be consulted in the planning stage and most of the contracts will go to the larger established and white voluntary organizations or the private sector.
- The move from grants to contracts will mean that voluntary organizations will increasingly need to focus on providing traditional services which reflect the status quo, and their ability to provide innovative services for previously ignored groups of people will be limited.

Equality of opportunity in employment

As we have already said the need to address equality of opportunity was recognized by the introduction of sex and racial discrimination legislation. Yet despite the existence of this legislation the employment positions of disadvantaged groups in our society have not markedly improved. Whilst more women and people from minority ethnic groups are found in the workforce, they still tend to be concentrated at the bottom of organizational hierarchies (for example, *see* Table 4.1). An EOC report (Stone, 1988) comments that in local authorities women tend to be concentrated in:

— 'women's' services
— lower-status jobs

— lower-paid jobs
— part-time jobs

Similar comments are likely to apply to ethnic minority employment.

Table 4.1: Civil servants by grade, sex and ethnic origin 1986–87

London and the South East of England — Percentages

Grade	White		Ethnic minority	
	Women	Men	Women	Men
Administrative Assistant	30.3	6.6	42.0	15.8
Administrative Officer	39.6	19.0	45.9	40.0
Executive Officer	20.9	31.1	10.2	27.8
Higher Executive Officer/Senior Executive Officer	7.4	30.2	1.6	13.0
Open Structure grades 4–7	1.8	12.5	0.4	3.4
Open Structure grades 1–3	—	0.5	—	—
Total	100	100	100	100

Source: *Women and Men in Britain: A Research Profile* (1988) HMSO, Table 6.9, p. 69.

What is the position of women and black people within your own organization? How are they distributed throughout the organizational hierarchy? Is this information readily available from your equal opportunities unit or personnel department? If not, why not? Is the composition of your workforce monitored in any other way — by age, disability, etc. Having constructed a picture of the distribution of staff within your organization, write down some comments on where the greatest inequality appears to lie.

We shall be focusing in the section 'Improving equality of opportunity' on ways in which equality of opportunity might be improved. First let us focus more specifically on why such inequality exists. One argument could be that past discrimination, which takes time to work through the system, is the cause of present disadvantage. The argument is that groups which have previously suffered from discrimination are not able to compete on an equal footing because of previous disadvantage. Positive action initiatives, such as special training schemes, are then proposed as one way of trying to compensate for previous discrimination. Where there have been few or no members of one sex (or racial group) in particular work in their employment for the previous twelve months, legislation allows employers to give special encouragement to, and provide specific training for, the minority sex (or racial group). Such measures are usually described as positive action. This is different to positive discrimination (which is illegal) where people are selected for employment or promotion because of their sex (or racial group).

It is, however, wishful thinking to believe that discrimination no longer occurs. Current discrimination is based on deeply ingrained attitudes and stereotypes which are difficult to dislodge. Torrington and Hall (1987, p.290) consider the preconceptions which affect the employment of people from disadvantaged groups.

These include:

- Ideas that women should not work because their place is in the home or with children (although this idea has much less support these days); that women do not want too much responsibility at work because of their home commitments; that you cannot move a woman to the other end of the country if her husband works at this end.
- Ideas that Sikhs or Moslems are difficult to employ because of problems with religious holidays and practices; that Indians or Pakistanis overstate their qualifications; that qualifications gained abroad are not as good as those gained in this country; that employees would not want to work for a black supervisor; that the ability to fill out an application form in good English is an indication of an individual's potential to do a manual job.
- Ideas that a person in a wheelchair will be an embarrassment to other workers; that a person in a wheelchair is in some way mentally disadvantaged/ abnormal; that someone who has suffered from mental illness will automatically crack up under the slightest pressure; that workers would not be able/wish to cope with someone suffering from epilepsy in case he or she had a fit at work.
- Ideas that older people are less adaptable; that they are not interested in coping with new technology; that they work much more slowly and cannot keep up with the pace of things; that they have become less interested in their careers

Such stereotypes can be very damaging. An EOC (undated) report on a collaborative exercise between themselves and the Metropolitan Police found that:

> discrimination was not always overt, intentional nor vindictive. Acts of discrimination were sometimes done with 'the best of intentions' or out of habit; for example, preventing women from being in the 'front line' during outbreaks of public disorder, because of a belief that women should be protected and not exposed to danger. This might be seen as chivalrous by some male officers, but took no account of the abilities of individual women or men and was liable seriously to inhibit women's policing experience and therefore their access to specialist and promotional posts.

As a result of applying such stereotypes disadvantaged groups end up being concentrated in lower-paid/lower-status jobs. Jobs become segregated; thus nursing is frequently seen as a job for women and medicine as a career for men.

It is wrong to place the problem of discrimination purely on the shoulders of individual prejudice. Husband (1991, p. 24) points out that:

> When we reduce racism and racial discrimination against ethnic minorities to prejudice, we are inevitably led to that analysis of the prejudiced person, since they are the 'problem'. Hence the policies which follow from this approach peripheralise the role of the

institutions of the state and the routine discriminatory practices which
are to be found in professions and other social institutions

The routinization of discriminatory practices institutionalizes them and they
become separate from and work independently of any single individual's prejudice.
Hence we can talk about institutional racism and institutional sexism.

One of the arguments for the continuing disadvantage of minority ethnic groups is
that their role is to provide a reserve army of labour. In advanced market economies
domestic shortages of labour in the post-Second World War period were resolved by
encouraging migrant labour from outside national boundaries — Britain looked to
its colonies. Together with married women, these originally migrant workers are
said to constitute a labour reserve to be used or discarded as the employment of
other groups rises or falls.

Other explanations of the continuation of disadvantage look at organizational
practices as well as individual attitudes. For example a Local Government
Operations Research Unit report (LGORU, 1982) offers three main reasons for the
present position of women in the workforce:

- *Organizational barriers* — women frequently have a career break to have children and then find it hard to re-enter organizations, particularly at the level at which they left.
- *Poor career planning* — on the part of women, and poor career counselling by organizations. Women often end up in dead end jobs.
- *Attitudes* — the low expectation some men have of women and the low expectations some women have of themselves.

Refer back to the previous exercise where you constructed a picture of the distribution of staff in your own organization. What appear to be the contributory factors which might explain why an unequal distribution of staff exists?

Equality of opportunity and access for service users

A family doctor in a joint practice refers all black patients to the Indian doctor at the practice, solely because of their colour and not because of their particular needs.

An optician instructs his receptionist not to register any more patients from a particular locality because of the large proportion of Africans living there.

Afro-Caribbean people presenting symptoms of cancer are prescribed aspirin because the GP does not take the time to reach a proper diagnosis.

These examples were reported in the *Health Service Journal* in February 1992 as an
introduction to its article on 'The Code of Practice in Primary Care Services',
published by the Commission for Racial Equality.

One thing to make clear from the start is that equality of opportunity does not mean
providing a standard service and saying that it is open to all. A simple example will

demonstrate why this is so. A library service is based on the first floor of a building in a city centre. It is open to all members of the public. Is there equality of opportunity and access for all members of the public? There is unlikely to be. People with a physical disability may find it difficult to come to the library, whilst those whose day-to-day activities may not bring them into the city centre may find it difficult or too expensive to use the facilities. Maybe what they find when they get there is that the material that everyone has an equal right to use is based around the reading tastes of the white middle class whose first language is English, hence their experience is one of being excluded. Whilst not directly discriminating, indirectly certain groups are disadvantaged by the service provided. Many people will claim that they are 'colour blind' and that the colour of a person's skin is immaterial to them. Whilst this may seem laudable (if it is true), its effects are pernicious in that it is likely to mean that all people are treated as if they were white. Any particular needs they have because of their ethnic origin are being ignored. A final example which may help you to understand the point we are trying to make comes from the Probation Service. An HM Inspectorate of Probation report (1991) makes the distinction between 'paper' justice and 'real' justice (they also use the phrases 'legal equality' as opposed to 'substantive equality'). The report (p. 59) points out that:

> 'paper' justice involves giving like penalties to women and men for like offences but 'real' justice involves taking into account the impact of a penalty: for example, at present women earn less than men, they carry the major responsibility for child-rearing

and

> The small number of women who have committed serious offences inhibits the development of adequate group facilities for them in most areas. It is not usually viable to include a minority of women in male-dominated schedule 11 groups.

Consider the services provided by your own organization. What possible sources of discrimination (direct or indirect) exist in relation to service use? Look for evidence of inequality in the following areas: low take-up rates for services amongst certain groups; inappropriate services or gaps in services for certain groups; the experience of discrimination in service delivery.

Research on the extent of equality of opportunity and access in public sector service delivery is not encouraging. Both direct and indirect discrimination are still rife. Some examples of research in this area will demonstrate the point.

In 1980 the Black Report on Inequality in Health Care was published. This was updated by the Health Divide in 1988. Both reports found inequalities in health relating to occupational grouping, social class, gender and ethnicity. Much of this inequality was found to relate to socio-economic status, rather than great inequalities in service delivery. Nevertheless there is no room for complacency as the following quotation demonstrates:

Studies have highlighted examples of poorer provision of services in more deprived areas; physical access difficulties for a small proportion of the population — notably among the elderly and manual groups; differences in the quality of care which appeared to favour higher occupational classes; and much lower uptake of preventive services by lower social groups (Whitehead, 1988, p. 273).

In 1982 the Commission for Racial Equality reported on a general investigation into the policies and practices of local authority housing departments towards applications for council housing from work permit holders living and working in the UK. This revealed that three local authorities in London were indirectly discriminating against homeless families or waiting-list applicants who were work permit holders by refusing to offer them permanent accommodation.

In 1985 the Commission for Racial Equality reported on a formal investigation in Birmingham LEA and found that Afro-Caribbean pupils were four times more likely to be suspended from secondary schools than white pupils for similar offences.

In 1985 a Commission for Racial Equality general investigation into the lending policies and practices of the local authority and building societies in Rochdale found widespread use of 'rule of thumb' practices that could indirectly discriminate against ethnic minority buyers.

In 1988 the Equal Opportunities Commission reported on a formal investigation into primary and secondary schools in West Glamorgan. They found that there was sex discrimination in the process of gaining access to craft subjects.

A 1990 report from the Commission for Racial Equality considered the roles of the Crown Prosecution Service and the Probation Service in making bail decisions, arguing the need to ensure that ethnic minority groups are not discriminated against in receiving custody rather than bail.

In order to give you a flavour of the way in which public sector services need to give attention to the multicultural nature of their customer/client groups and the implications of this for the sorts of service they deliver, Case study 4.1 describes the way in which racial discrimination occurred in one Further Education College providing a nursery nursing course (NNEB).

Case Study 4.1

This case involves a College of Further Education in the Midlands. The college has been in existence for about fifty years under a succession of names and forms of organization. It is in a middle-class suburb which has always been predominantly white but which is undergoing demographic changes and is beginning to reflect the multicultural nature of the city. Many of the staff live fairly close to the college: some of them have worked there for twenty years or more. Traditionally, most of the students come from the local schools and are aged 16 to 19. The college has always prided itself on its close links with its feeder schools and on its good examination results. It has always provided vocational as well as 'academic' courses, and has run the NNEB course very successfully for over twenty years. It has recently been considering the introduction of innovatory courses like BTEC and is trying to recruit more mature students.

Last September, an Afro-Caribbean woman aged 31 enrolled on the NNEB course. Her group consisted of one Asian student, eleven white students and two Afro-Caribbean students, including Joyce herself. All five tutors on the course were white women, ranging in age from mid-twenties to late fifties. Two of them had been engaged on the course since it started years ago.

A week or so after term started, Joyce formed the opinion that the course was being taught in an overtly Eurocentric fashion. Handouts from tutors contained remarks like: 'a new-born baby should be a healthy pink colour', and 'breathing difficulties may make the lips look blue'. When Joyce pointed out that these statements were not true of black people her objections were shrugged aside. She was told that the notes reflected the syllabus, and if she wanted to pass the exam she must learn these 'facts'.

In the second half-term students were required to do an in-depth study of a common disease — its frequency, symptoms, causes and treatment. Joyce decided to study sickle-cell anaemia. She was told that this was not appropriate, since it was not a common disease in this country. She pointed out that very many Afro-Caribbean women suffer from it, and that anyone engaged in any kind of social work in Birmingham ought to know about it. Again, she was referred to the syllabus, which gave a list of examples of diseases. She was told that this list was definitive, although it clearly was not.

As the course continued, Joyce found herself constantly arguing for a multicultural approach. Subjects of dispute included children's stories and rhymes, diet, domestic routines, family structures and body language. In each case, Joyce demanded recognition that the white middle-class version was not the only version, or the norm by which other versions should be measured. Whenever she introduced her views she was stopped by the tutor on the grounds that she was demanding things not on the syllabus and was wasting the group's time. She had the impression that the two younger tutors were sympathetic to her, but were being overruled by their senior colleagues. All but one of the other students (a white woman) took the part of the tutors, and demanded that Joyce should shut up and follow the course as it stood. One woman in particular accused Joyce of deliberate sabotage of the group and of black activism. Several unpleasant arguments took place within the group, both inside and outside the classroom.

Meanwhile, rumours about the unhappiness of the group had spread round the college. Joyce found herself being treated rudely by canteen staff and porters, one of whom objected to a piece of jewellery she was wearing on the grounds that 'You're not in Africa now'. She felt isolated and persecuted.

This state of affairs continued for two terms. Joyce had several interviews with senior members of staff and acquired a reputation for aggressive and violent behaviour. This arose because she wore her fingernails long, and when agitated would wag her finger at her antagonist. One man reported that she had glared at him like a tiger and he thought she was going to gouge his eyes out. Joyce herself emerged from the same meeting in tears because she had been constantly shouted down and 'treated as though she was in the dock'.

At the end of the second term Joyce was given two options: she could stay away from college for a term to 'cool off' and start from scratch in September, or she could join a parallel groups immediately and continue the course without a break if she undertook to stop raising black issues.

She tried the parallel group — under protest — but found that her reputation as a trouble-maker dogged her, and was unable to work. At the end of the academic year she had a nervous breakdown and abandoned her ambitions to get a vocational qualification.

Reprinted with the permission of the Commission for Racial Equality

Read through the case study and then consider the following questions:

1. *What examples of direct discrimination are to be found in this case study?*
2. *How does indirect discrimination manifest itself?*
3. *If you were the junior member of staff who sympathized with Joyce's point of view what action might you have taken?*
4. *Are there any examples of service delivery practice in your own organization which parallel the sort of discrimination found in this case study?*

We have already said that trying to define what is meant by equality is not easy. There is much debate as to whether equality in public policy means equality of opportunity, equality of utilization or equality of outcome (*see* LeGrand, 1982).

- Equality of opportunity may result in serious inequalities of outcome because some people are better equipped than others to take advantage of the opportunities available.
- It is also possible for there to be equality of access without equality of utilization. Some people may not perceive that they need the particular service.
- Equality of access is no guarantee of equality of outcome. Bevan (1990) asks the question, 'Providing equal access to health care may be thought equitable, but if, when patients get there, doctors do different things, is that equitable?'.

What concept of equality is used by your organization (equality of opportunity, equality of utilization, equality of outcome)? What difference would the adoption of different definitions make?

Improving equality of opportunity

There is no requirement in law to have an equal opportunities policy, although it is recommended. A survey of practice in local government was conducted by *Labour Research* in February 1988. An extract from of one of their summary tables is provided in Table 4.2. It shows that 84% of responding authorities said that they had an equal opportunities policy, but only half had a policy about monitoring the position with regard to this statement.

Table 4.2: *Number of councils with policies*

Policy	Yes	No
Equal opportunities	78 (84%)	13 (14%)
Monitoring	49 (53%)	37 (40%)
Statistics kept	61 (66%)	28 (30%)
Job share scheme	38 (41%)	49 (53%)
Nursery/crèche provision	16 (17%)	71 (77%)
Childcare payments	3 (3%)	77 (84%)
Family leave	43 (46%)	43 (46%)
Training schemes	37 (40%)	53 (57%)
Sexual harassment	37 (40%)	53 (57%)

Note: Figures do not add up to 100 per cent as some authorities did not respond to the particular question.

Source: Labour Research, February, 1988.

A survey of practice in the NHS conducted by the EOC (EOC, *c* 1990) found that:

- 93% of Health Authorities and Boards state that they have an equal opportunities statement or policy, but 10% have not committed their policy to paper.
- 30% have not communicated the policy to their employees.
- 78% of policies fail to mention sexual harassment.
- 60% do not have an equal opportunities committee to plan or evaluate progress.
- 84% have not appointed a manager whose chief responsibility is the maximizing of human resources through the development of equal opportunities.
- 75% do not monitor their policy and no Health Authority monitors the position of women with children.

There are differing views as to how discrimination might be countered. There is the legislative approach which aims to 'outlaw' discrimination; so far this has been the predominant approach. Another approach stresses the primacy of attitudinal change and the importance of training, arguing that things will only truly change if there are fundamental changes in the attitudes towards people of differing racial backgrounds, women, the disabled, etc. There is support for this latter view in the fact that the review of the effectiveness of the equal opportunities legislation to date is not encouraging. The two approaches are not mutually exclusive and arguably they should be used together.

The Equal Opportunities Commission (working on sex discrimination) and the Commission for Racial Equality both produce very useful documents on anti-discriminatory practice. A simplified step-by-step process for addressing equal opportunities is:

- Formulate a policy
  — consult with employees and their representatives
  — establish a policy
  — communicate that policy to all employees
  — allocate responsibility for implementing policy
- Implement policy
  — work out a strategy for implementing policy
  — examine existing procedures and practices
  — establish required procedures and practices
  — provide training (including positive action)
- Monitor policy
  — collect information
  — monitor and review the implementation process and its effects

Where organizations have an equal opportunities policy this may not be readily apparent in practice, as the following quotation from an NHS employee demonstrates:

> The Authority claims to be an equal opportunity employer and commits itself to '... take positive action to promote equal opportunities and facilities for disabled and other disadvantaged groups'. The policy is striking for the number of statements of action which are not actually carried out and is apposite in demonstrating the gap which can exist between policy and practice.

In part this may be due to the fact that equality of opportunity is competing with a large agenda of other changes. In the main, however, the difficulty of moving from policy to practice lies in the entrenched attitudes and values of those involved. Preconceptions of various workers' abilities are difficult to counter. A manager within a central government department commented that:

> In reality (despite the equal opportunities slot on most training courses) amongst all grades stereotyping still abounds and by implication prejudice is also alive and well. Unfortunately the blandness of the existing equal opportunities policies makes their penalties easy to avoid providing there is no overt prejudicial behaviour.

Clearly having an equal opportunities policy statement is not enough, an implementation strategy is all-important. Such a strategy should outline the concrete steps which can be taken to address possible discriminatory practice in areas such as:

— staff recruitment
— staff promotion
— training and development opportunities
— access to services
— the experience and relevance of services

An implementation strategy should develop into an action plan which specifies what is going to happen, by when it is going to happen, and who is responsible for making it happen. Some form of quantitative analysis of present practices may help in identifying where action is needed. In a very useful book by Coussey and Jackson (1991) an example is provided of analysing where action is needed in the recruitment process. The series of questions which need to be answered are set out in Figure 4.1.

What action has your organization taken in relation to addressing possible discriminatory practices in recruitment, promotion and staff development? Has it done anything in relation to possible discrimination in service delivery?

Strategies for change need to focus on the barriers to equality of opportunity. For example, a number of strategies have been proposed to address the barriers for women at work:

- Provide better accommodation of the career break (legislation on maternity leave has helped)
    — Keep women in touch via part-time work at convenient hours
    — Make sure that you are not setting inappropriate age limits (e.g. Civil Service age limit of 28 years for recruitment of Executive Officers was found by an Industrial Tribunal to be indirect discrimination against women)
    — Provide crèche facilities to enable women to go back to work earlier
- Try to eliminate direct or indirect discrimination in organizational practices — particularly in relation to recruitment and promotions
- Help women to overcome their own barriers
    — raise expectations/confidence
    — help with guilt complex of leaving children
    — encourage more women to move into positions of responsibility
    — provide career planning sessions

As well as establishing rules and guidelines, a strategy document is also likely to consider how awareness of equal opportunities issues can be improved. Training has a key role to play in this latter area.

Many would argue that statements about trying to achieve progress are insufficient without at the same time establishing targets. Targets are different from quotas, which are illegal in Britain (except in relation to disability). Targets need to be set at levels which are realistic but which also pose a challenge. Whilst they are advantageous, they can be seen as the maximum to be achieved rather than as a starting point.

Figure 4.1: *Identifying where action is needed in the recruitment process*

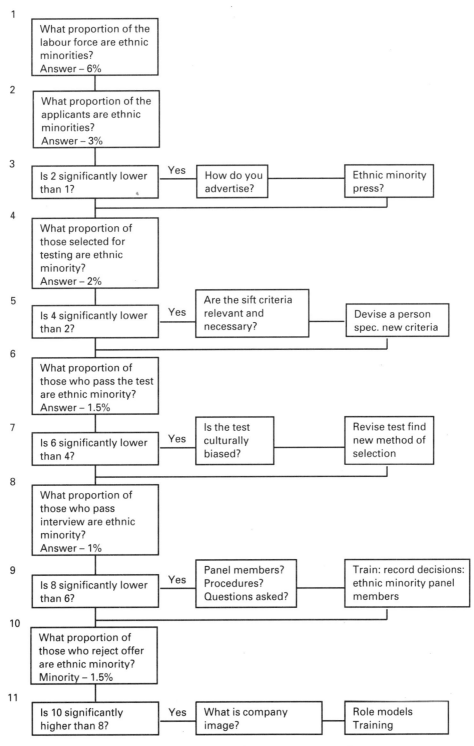

Source: Coussey & Jackson (1991) *Making Equal Opportunities Work* Pitman

In order to be able to assess the present situation and monitor the effectiveness of proposed action, equal opportunities policies and strategies frequently identify and categorize various disadvantaged groups. An example of such a classification system is that used by the Commission for Racial Equality and the 1991 Census for identifying ethnic origin:

— White
— Black — African
— Black — Caribbean
— Black — other
— Indian
— Pakistani
— Bangladeshi
— Chinese
— Other (please describe)

Whilst in many instances classification is useful, it is important to remember that such categories are not mutually exclusive. A disabled person has a gender and belongs to an ethnic group and should not be 'treated' solely on the basis of their disability. The labelling of disadvantage may mean that the needs of certain groups are ignored — for example, disabled black people and black women. An EOC survey of Equal Opportunities in Local Authorities (Stone, 1988) found that there was 'considerable concern about the way in which equal opportunities initiatives had failed to reflect the particular needs of Black women'.

There is also the question as to who implements such a classification system and how the data is collected. Do you get employees to self-classify or do you ask managers to do this on their behalf?

Refer back to the exercise in the section 'Equality of opportunity in employment' on the position of women and black people within your own organization. Is enough being done to try and improve this picture? How would you quicken the pace of change?

So far this section has considered improving equality of opportunity as if it could be treated rationally and objectively: collect information, establish goals and policies for change, allocate responsibility, produce an implementation strategy, monitor and review progress. In Chapter 3 on power and influence we stressed the importance of considering organizations as coalitions of interest and the management process as one of influencing, negotiation and bargaining. Many would argue that one of the reasons for the continuing disadvantage of certain groups in our society is that it is in the interest of those groups which have power to maintain the status quo. Whilst lip service might be paid to equality of opportunity, it is argued, there is no intention of altering the current distribution of power in society. Thus whilst those concerned with promoting equality of opportunity need to follow an 'up front' activity which emphasizes the rational processes and arguments outlined above, at the same time they need to consider the distribution of power and how they can influence others and establish counter-coalitions. This distinction between 'up front' and 'backstage' activity is explored further in Chapter 12 on managing change.

Conclusions

This chapter began by saying that working for equal opportunities should be a concern for all managers. It then went on to place this concern in context by considering the extent of inequality, why it exists and how it might be addressed. It ended up by considering the main steps by which organizations seek to improve equality: by establishing policies, devising an implementation strategy, monitoring and reviewing progress.

As a result of this discussion it is likely that two main concerns will feature on your own equal opportunities agenda:

1. increasing your understanding of the assumptions and values which may underpin your own behaviour and work practice
2. encouraging your organization to consider its policies and practices by constantly ensuring that equal opportunity issues are identified and addressed.

Neither of these courses of action is easy. Those who vigorously try to improve equal opportunities will need energy, tenacity, understanding and political skills. The task will not be easy, but the goal is very worthwhile.

References

ANGLE, H.L. and PERRY, J.L. (1981) 'An Empirical Assessment of Organisational Commitment and Organisational Effectiveness', *Administrative Science Quarterly*, **26**, 1–14.

BEVAN, G. (1990) 'Equity and variability in modern health care', in T.F. ANDERSON and G. MOONEY, *The Challenges of Medical Practice Variations*, Macmillan.

COUSSEY, M. and JACKSON, H. (1991) *Making Equal Opportunities Work*, Pitman.

EOC (c1988) *Formal Investigation Report: West Glamorgan Schools*, Equal Opportunities Commission.

EOC (1990) *Equality Management: Women's Employment in the NHS*, Equal Opportunities Commission.

EOC (undated) *Managing to make progress: A report of a collaborative exercise between the Metropolitan Police and the Equal Opportunities Commission*, Metropolitan Police District, New Scotland Yard.

FRYER, P. (1989) *Black People in the British Empire: An Introduction*, Pluto Press.

HM INSPECTORATE OF PROBATION (1991) *Report on Women Offenders and Probation Service Provision*, Home Office.

HMSO (1988) *Women and Men in Britain: A Research Profile*, HMSO.

HOMANS, H. (1987) 'Man-made Myths: The Reality of Being a Woman Scientist in the NHS' in A. SPENCER and D. PODMORE (eds.), *In a Man's World*, Tavistock.

HUSBAND, C. (1991) quoted in *One Small Step Towards Racial Justice*, Central Council for Education and Training in Social Work, p. 24.

LEGRAND, J. (1982) *The Strategy of Equality*, Allen & Unwin.

LGORU (1982) *Women in Local Government, the Neglected Resource*, Report No. P1, Local Government Operations Research Unit.

MULLARD, C. (1991) 'Towards a Model of Anti racist Social Work', in *One Small Step Towards Racial Justice*, Central Council for Education and Training in Social Work.

NCVO (1991) *Contracts for care: Issues for Black and Other Ethnic Minority Voluntary Groups*, National Council for Voluntary Organizations.

NCVO (1993) *Contracts in Black and White*, National Council for Voluntary Organizations.

RUBENSTEIN, M. (1987) 'Modern myths and misconception: "Equal opportunities makes good business sense', *Equal Opportunities Review*, November/December, p. 48.

STONE, I. (1988) *Equal Opportunities in Local Authorities: Developing effective strategies for the implementation of policies for women*, HMSO.

TORRINGTON, D. and HALL, L. (1987) *Personnel Management: A new approach*, Prentice-Hall.

WHITEHEAD, M. (1988) 'The Health Divide' published together with 'The Black Report' in *Inequalities in Health*, Penguin, 1990.

Guided reading

Explanations of legislative obligations and practical guidelines relating to the many aspects of reducing/eliminating race and sex discrimination can be obtained from:

Commission for Racial Equality, Headquarters, Elliot House, 10–12 Allington Street, London SW1E 5EH

Equal Opportunities Commission, Headquarters, Overseas House, Quay Street, Manchester, M3 3HN

A *Code of Good Practice on the employment of people with a disability* was published by the Department of Employment in 1988.

A good practical book on implementing equal opportunities policies and practices is COUSSEY, M. and JACKSON, H. (1991) *Making Equal Opportunities Work*, Pitman.

Issues of race and developing anti-racist practices are further explored in:

JACKSON, H. and FIELD, S. (1989) *Race, Community Groups and Service Delivery*, Home Office.

CONNELLY, N. (1989) *Race and Change in Social Services Departments*, Policy Studies Institute.

The role of women at work and the institutionalization of sexism is explored in COYLE, A. and SKINNER, J. (eds.) (1988) *Women and Work: Positive Action for Change*, Macmillan. A compendium of research evidence is provided in a forthcoming book by F. Wilson, to be published by McGraw-Hill.

Chapter 5:
Marketing public services

This chapter is intended to assist you in understanding what marketing is, and how it might be helpful for your service. By the end of the chapter you should:

- be clear about what is special about marketing;
- understand the components of a marketing strategy and its links to business planning;
- know how to utilize a marketing approach for your service.

What is marketing?

As always the best place to start is with your own knowledge. Write down your own definition of marketing.

Your definition may well have included some of the following aspects:

— selling a product/service
— packaging a product/service so as to enhance its selling potential
— advertising
— market research.

As will be seen below, all these, and more, are part of a marketing approach, but they are not its essence. **Marketing is concerned with the identification and satisfaction of customer or potential service user needs and preferences.** It involves a range of different activities including:

— market research
— product/service design
— pricing
— selling
— distribution
— promotion/advertising
— quality management
— evaluation.

For any public agency marketing means providing the *right service*, at the *right time*, in the *right place*, and at the *right price*. The focus of the whole process should be upon your service users, and so marketing is about a 'user-oriented' approach to service management. This requires you to be clear about exactly who your user, or users, are, and what they need.

Until a few years ago, few public services would consider marketing to be an appropriate activity for them. The consensus was that public services were outside the market, for good reasons, and so could plan in other ways.

However, the increasing costs of public services and awareness of the shortfalls in their management have led to a far more market-oriented approach to be adopted for service planning and distribution. Marketing is an essential part of this. Moreover, the introduction of the market, in various forms, into the provision of public services does mean that service managers now need to pay attention to such issues as pricing and promotion, which had not been previously considered in service planning.

Used properly, it is a powerful tool for planning your service to relate directly to the expressed needs of your service users and potential users. For it to be so powerful, it is important that a genuine 'marketing' approach is adopted. It is important to realize that marketing is not just selling a product or service, but is an integrated set of activities. This point is explored in more detail in the next section.

Selling and marketing orientations

A selling orientation starts with an existing service of your agency and uses promotional techniques to convince would-be users that this is what they want. These users are not participants in this process, but its recipients. In public sector terms, it is perhaps similar to a service-led approach to service delivery (i.e. fitting needs to existing services) rather than a needs-led one (i.e. designing service to meet expressed needs). It is illustrated in Figure 5.1.

Figure 5.1: *A selling orientation*

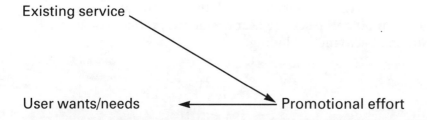

A **marketing orientation** by contrast, starts with identifying user wants/needs and then develops services in response to these. The role of promotion is to communicate this new service to potential customers, and to give feedback upon it. Ideally this should be followed by a re-evaluation of service user wants/needs. This is illustrated in Figure 5.2.

Marketing is thus a far more pro-active and participative process than selling, which is a linear and one-directional process. However, managers in the public sector may well, with some justification, argue that they already design services in response to users' needs, so that marketing is nothing new.

Figure 5.2: *A marketing orientation*

This is where a second characteristic of a marketing orientation comes in. This is that it takes place in *the market* and that service users and potential service users express their own preferences by 'voting with their feet', as to which public services they want, rather than having this defined by professionals or other public sector workers. Certainly the legislation of the last decade, such as the Local Government Act 1988 and NHS and Community Care Act 1992, have gone a long way to creating such a market for public services, as has the general trend toward privatization and competition. Supporters of this process would argue that it has strengthened the power of individual users of services to define their own needs. Opponents have argued that it has weakened their power, by disaggregating them into individuals, rather than responding to them as collectives of users who can exercise their power as a pressure group. What do you think?

Think about the differences between marketing and selling outlined above and then try to reply to the questions in the grid below. It may be helpful in doing this to think about how your organization would work using either a selling or marketing approach. A suggested contrast is included in Appendix 5.1 to this chapter.

What is the focus of organization?	What 'business' are you in?	To whom is the service directed?	What is your primary goal?	How do you seek to achieve this goal?

Characteristics of markets

Markets are constantly changing and a key part of marketing is to monitor these changes and to plan to meet them, rather than providing a pre-set range of goods/services, irrespective of market changes. The starting point for any marketing plan is to understand the characteristics of your market. These are sometimes called the 'Six Os':

Occupants: Who is the market?
Objects: What do they want?
Occasion: When do they want it?
Organization: Who is involved in making decisions upon these wants?
Objectives: Why do people want?
Operations: In what ways do people satisfy these wants?

The first three of these issues appear relatively straightforward (remembering that another agency might be your customer). However public sector organizations have not always been very good at deciding who their service users should be, or about the time-scale of their needs. Nor is it always clear exactly who your primary user is. Services have sometimes been provided to meet the time-scale of the organization, rather than the needs of the service users. A good example of this is a 'tuck-in' service for vulnerable elderly people in the community, which puts them to bed at a time to suit the service rota, rather than in relation to their own needs.

The fourth point, the decision-makers, is an important one for public sector organizations, as potential or actual service users do not necessarily have complete decision-making autonomy. Children have only limited choice in terms of their schooling, for example, because of the influence of the state (in terms of statutory legislation), their parents (in choosing a school) and their teachers (in terms of the curriculum). It is important therefore to be clear what the range of potential decision-makers is for any public sector service, and the range of decisions that each can have an effect upon.

Think about the market for your own organization, and make a list of its characteristics under the 'six Os'. Keep this for use in the next section, as it will form the starting-point for deciding upon your market segment.

The components of marketing

This section takes you through the key components of marketing. For each subsection you should consider the points in relation to your own organization, and keep a record of them on the chart in Appendix 5.2.

Goals and objectives

The starting point of any marketing strategy has to be some basic questions about your organization:

1. what is the purpose ('business') of your organization?
2. who are your primary service users?
3. what are the objectives that you need to meet to achieve your purpose?
4. what tasks/processes are central to these objectives?
5. what staff are required?

A difficulty for you may be that your agency has never thought through these issues clearly. It may be useful to go through these questions with your colleagues to clarify some of these issues, then complete the first section of Appendix 5.2. Make a note of any disagreements.

Market segmentation

It is unlikely that any particular service is going to be needed by everyone. It is important therefore to identify the *target population* of your organization. Unless you do this, contact with the wider population will be unnecessarily expensive, and, moreover, at a later stage you will need to filter out people from outside this target group. This will increase your costs unnecessarily. An important tool in this process is market research, which is discussed in more detail in the next subsection, below. The focus here is upon the broad parameters of your market segment.

Usually, you will need to consider three categories in deciding your market segment, starting with the total 'markets' you identified the section on 'Characteristics of markets' above.

Geography

Think about the following:

1. what are the geographic boundaries of your service (e.g. town/county/region)?
2. are there specific characteristics of this area which need to be taken into consideration (e.g. urban/rural character)?
3. does the geography of your area require any special resources (e.g. transport in a remote, sparsely populated area)?

Demography

Think about the following:

1. what are the key demographic factors of your target population?

These can include
— size of the target group
— age/gender
— income/occupation
— cultural background
— ethnic make-up of group

Many of these will be easily accessible through the existing information gathered by your own agency, or another one (such as the Office of Population Censuses and Surveys). For others you may need to design specific market research, as detailed below.

Specific needs

Think about the following:

1. are there issues of access (such as for disabled people), or image (is the service seen as one only for the poor, which could deter some people from applying) which need to be taken into account?
2. how stable is your market segment, or is it open to change (either demographically based, or resulting from the intrusion of a competitor agency)?

3. are there any aspects of the lifestyle of your target group which need to be taken into account?

Market research

The purpose of this is to decide how much demand there is for a specific public service and to provide you with important information in developing your market segment and marketing mix (*see below*). You need to establish what your potential users need and want (which may not be the same thing!), and to decide whether this is an appropriate target for your agency.

The sort of questions that market research (MR) can address are:

1. what is the size of the total market for a service, and is this changing in any direction (for example, is the frail elderly population in your area increasing or decreasing, in relation to the demand for home care services)?
2. what should be your target, the whole market or just a segment of it (is a health promotion unit going to try and reduce smoking by all women or target teenage girls as its priority)?
3. where are your potential users located and where should the service be located (does it need to be centralized or decentralized — and if so where to)?
4. who will make the decision to purchase a service (the user, a relative, or another agency)?
5. who are your potential competitors/collaborators?

There are three sources of MR. These are

— primary research
— secondary research
— organizational analysis.

Primary research

This involves actually going out and finding out about the needs of your potential users, by direct contact. This may involve:

— questionnaires (both in person and by post);
— pilot projects;
— visits to other agencies;
— observation of an agency similar to your own.

The important point here is not just to collect any information, but to be clear from the outset what information you need in order to make your marketing decisions; how you are going to collect it; and how you are going to analyse it/make decisions upon it. Obviously the more comprehensive/sophisticated is your research, the more useful it is likely to be for decision-making, but also the more costly. You need to decide on the correct balance for your service.

Finally this type of research is fraught with difficulties and biases, if not constructed properly. Even an apparently simple task such as framing a question on a questionnaire can introduce bias into the answer. People often like to agree with the person to whom they are speaking, and if there is an implicit bias in a question, then this will affect your results. For example, the question, 'Why is television bad for children' includes the assumption that it is bad, rather than leaving the question open. In MR it is therefore important to consult one of the many standard texts on study design, a few of which are named at the end of this chapter.

Secondary research

This involves the use of existing information services, and is particularly useful for demographic trends. It can include:

- government publications, such as Family Expenditure Survey or General Household Survey
- local government statistics, such as the size and needs of the local population of people with learning disabilities
- specialist research reports from respected institutions, such as the Policy Studies Institute or the King's Fund

Organizational analysis

It is also important to be aware of the potential and weaknesses of your own organization. A useful tool here is the SWOT analysis. This means looking at your agency in terms of:

— internal *strengths*
— internal *weaknesses*
— external *opportunities* for growth and development
— external *threats* to its work and continuance.

Marketing mix

This is the centre of your marketing strategy. It involves blending the variables of your service in a way that best meets the needs of your potential service users, in the market segment that you have outlined above. The key variables of this mix are:

— product/service design
— price
— promotion
— place

They are discussed in more detail in the subsections below.

Product/service design

This involves bringing together all the key aspects of the product/service of your agency. The key issues at this stage are:

- Relevance — does the service meet the expressed needs of your service users?

- Quality/performance — is the service of the quality wanted by your service users, and what systems do you have to assure/control the quality?
- Identity — does your service have a clear identity for your service users, so that they can recognize how it meets their needs?
- Features — does your service require only one standard mode of delivery, or do you need a range of optional modes for different service users, or even the ability to adapt the service to each individual user?
- Design — is the service welcoming and does it encourage the target group to use it, and how do you ensure that it is not misused by people outside this target group (gate-keeping)?
- 'Warranty' — what guarantees/safeguards do you offer to your service users about their safety and what processes are available for complaints?
- Access — is the service readily available to your target group, or what subsystems do you need to establish (such as transport or support services) in order to ensure easy access?

Think about your own service. Did it take these issues into account in its design, and if so how successful is it? If it did not, how would you go about considering them, and what might the impact be? Might there be any drawbacks as well as advantages to this approach?

Pricing

It is sometimes assumed that pricing has no place in public services because they are funded indirectly, through taxation. This is no longer as true as it used to be however, so prices are increasingly being introduced for public services. Examples of this trend are a fee to join a music lending department of a public library, and a charge for the pest removal service of the local authority. Moreover, your own agency may well be selling services to another public agency, where a price does need to be approved. This is increasingly the case within the Health Service, for example.

Issues of costing are covered in more detail in a separate chapter (Chapter 10). However, you will need to take the following factors into account in considering your pricing strategy:

- Price level — what is the right price for the potential users in your market segment, in terms of what they are prepared to pay for it? is this a sustainable price for your agency (i.e. does it meet your costs)? how does it compare to the prices of your competitors? does your price say anything about your service that you want said (such as that it is 'value for money')?

- Special arrangements   do you need to consider any form of vouchers or free passes for the service to encourage access?
  should you have any special arrangements for 'bulk purchases', particularly if by another agency?
- Arrangement for payment   do you need alternative forms of payment and if so what should they be?
  are the terms for payment clear and understandable?
  what will happen in the event of non-payment?
- Changes   how are changes in prices to be arranged/negotiated?
  do you need a clear policy on changes in advance or should they be worked out as they happen?
  what processes are necessary to communicate price changes?

It is also important that, particularly for public services, there can be other costs, besides the price of a service, that your potential users need to consider. These can be as influential as the actual price of the service in their decision-making. The most common of these are:-

- *Opportunity costs* — If someone is using your service, they are forgoing the opportunity to use other services? A person using a leisure centre in the evening is forgoing the opportunity to use adult education classes at the same time, for example. Those sorts of costs cannot really be included in your price, but you need to be aware of them, particularly in deciding the time and place of your service, to avoid clashes with other important services for your target group.
- *Embarrassment costs* — These are incurred by your users when your service is seen as stigmatizing, either because of the process of application (such as proving that you are one of the 'deserving' rather than 'undeserving' poor, in terms of benefit), or because the service in itself is seen to be stigmatizing, as is often the case with state benefits for unemployed people. Again, you need to decide how you are going to challenge and/or minimize such embarrassment.

Does your agency have a pricing policy? What impact does it have upon access to your agency, and what message does it give about it in terms of image? If your agency does not have a policy, talk to your senior managers and find out why it is not appropriate. What impact might the introduction of one have? If you do have a policy, what is its impact? Can you suggest any modifications?

Promotion

The importance of promotion is to *communicate* the nature and availability of your service to the target group. The most common form of promotion is by *advertising* through the media such as the press, television, radio and outdoor advertising (including static posters and leaflet distribution). The issue here is to make sure that your chosen media is focused upon your target group, rather than the population in general. For example, if you are targeting a service for the West Indian community in your area, then it could make more sense to use the local West Indian community paper, if there is one, rather than the general press.

In designing an advertisement of any type it must:

A — attract **attention** from the target group
I — be **interesting** and cover the major features of the service
D — be **desirable** to potential service users by showing how it matches their expressed needs
A — be **action**-oriented by giving potential service users enough information to find/gain access to your service.

Using these principles, design an advertisement for your service. Show it to your colleagues and/or existing service users. What do they think? How might you improve it? Alternatively review the existing advertisements for your service against the above criteria. How effective are they?

However, if advertising is the most common form of promotion, it is not the sole one. Others include:

1. direct contacts with potential service users, by home visits or public meetings;
2. mail delivery or leaflet distribution to your target group;
3. brochure/other literature explaining the service (remembering what languages it will need to be in);
4. promotional events, such as public openings or open days.

You need to decide the best promotional strategy for your service, based upon the need to gain the attention of your target group. Again, either review your existing promotional strategy and recommend improvements, or design one, if there is not one already in place.

Place/distribution

The final choice to be made in your marketing mix is where to situate your service;

1. if it is for a specific community (such as an Asian community) should it be within that community?
2. if it is for a group with a specific problem, such as a physical disability or lack of transport, how is access to be ensured?
3. do you need one central service point, such as as resource centre, or multiple outlets, such as branch/mobile libraries?

Marketing overview

To summarize the marketing process, once you have clarified a *market and/or market segment* for your agency, you need to develop a *marketing strategy* to ensure that the needs of this target group are met. This strategy will be composed of a blend of the four variables which form your *marketing mix*.

This chapter has taken you through the various stages and techniques of marketing, and demonstrated how it might be useful for public sector organizations. At its centre are the service users (and potential service users) of your organization, as the key determinant of your service. The process is illustrated in Figure 5.3. The latter stage, of service evaluation is covered in Chapters 8 and 9, on managing performance and quality.

Figure 5.3: *The marketing process*

```
┌──────────────────────────┐
▼                          │
Market research            │
│                          │
▼                          │
Choice of market/market segment
│                          │
▼                          │
Clarification of marketing mix
│                          │
▼                          │
Development of marketing strategy
│                          │
▼                          │
Service delivery           │
│                          │
▼                          │
Evaluation ────────────────┘
```

Always remember that this is a circular, not one-way process. Marketing and MR is not a once and for all process, but an iterative one.

Beyond marketing: business planning

It is sometimes the case that marketing and business planning are spoken of as if they were the same thing. They are not. Business planning carries on from your marketing plan to fit this into crucial resource issues. The most important of these are:

— income and expenditure forecasts
— cash flow plans
— capital investment
— allocation of human resources

If marketing is about what is *desirable* in terms of a service, then business planning is about what is *feasible*, within your resources.

In all likelihood, business planning will be done at a senior level in your agency, as it will require key strategic decisions to be taken about the purpose and thrust of your agency, and its relationship(s) to your competitors/collaborators. However, it is important for you to understand how your own marketing plan fits into the business plan of your agency as a whole. Moreover, as public agencies become increasingly decentralized, you may well need to consider simple business planning for your unit or service.

Content of a business plan

There is no set format for a business plan, but it should always cover the following issues:

- *aims of the agency* — these should have been clarified as part of your marketing plan, as should any potential conflicts in them.
- *agency environment* — broadly this is how your agency relates to its environment as a whole. You will already have considered this in part, when conducting your market research. However, in a business plan you do need to consider the wider context of your agency. This includes changes in the social and economic environment of your agency, as well as the plans and actions of other agencies in your field. In a market it is very important to know your competitors' plans as well as your own.
- *service objectives* — this should be a clear summary of the marketing plan that you have already designed. It should specify what your target market is, in terms of potential service users, what products/services you intend to provide for them (outputs), and with what intended outcomes.
- *evaluation plan* — this should link the above outputs and outcomes to an ongoing plan designed to monitor the efficacy and effectiveness of your service. This is discussed in more detail in Chapter 8, below.
- *resource plan* — this will include your income and expenditure budgets, and human resource allocations, indicating how resources are to be used in translating the 'desirable' market plan into 'feasible' reality. In the private sector this would include the forecasting of potential profits and losses, but these may be less relevant in public agencies. The key here is the actual resources needed to meet your organizational aims.

The business plan may also need an appendix, detailing any underlying assumptions that you have made and which are not already apparent. It could also include a contingency plan to deal with any foreseen (or even unforeseen!) difficulties.

Conclusions

This section has taken you through the process of developing a marketing plan, and illustrated briefly its links with business planning. This should have allowed you to monitor the position of your own agency in terms of being prepared for a more market-based approach to delivering public services. The next chapter will go on to explore how you might develop new services upon the basis of your marketing

Appendix 5.1: *The marketing and selling orientations*

	THE ORGANIZATION'S FOCUS IS:	WHAT BUSINESS ARE YOU IN?	TO WHOM IS THE SERVICE DIRECTED?	WHAT IS YOUR PRIMARY GOAL?	HOW DO YOU SEEK TO ACHIEVE YOUR GOAL?
SELLING ORIENTATION	Inward upon the organization's needs	Delivering programs and services	Everybody	Maximum numbers through the door	Primarily through intensive promotion
MARKETING ORIENTATION	Outward upon the wants and preferences of user groups	Satisfying user wants	Specific groups of people	User satisfaction	Through co-ordinated use of the set of marketing activities

Source: adapted from J. Crompton and C. Lamb (1988) *Marketing Government and Social Services*, Wiley.

plan, whilst Part 3 of this book will look at some of the issues involved in the operational management of services. The key to all these processes, however, is robust and realistic marketing and business plans which clarify your objectives, service intentions and expected outcomes.

Appendix 5.2:

Marketing strategy pro-forma

Use these headings to pull together your answers to the exercises in this chapter, and then to consider what the implications are for your service. Discuss these with your colleagues and line manager.

1. **Goals and objectives of your organization**
Write down the answers to questions listed in the section on 'goals and objectives'.

2. **Market segmentation**

3. **Marketing mix**
   i) Product strategy
   ii) Pricing
   iii) Promotion
   iv) Place

Guided reading

The following are all good overall texts upon marketing in the public and non-profit sectors.

CROMPTON, J. and LAMB, C. (1988) *Marketing Government and Social Services*, Wiley.

KOTLER, P. and ANDREASON, A. (1987) *Strategic Marketing for NonProfit Organizations*, Prentice-Hall.

LAUFFER, A. (1984) *Strategic Marketing for Not for Profit Organizations*, Free Press.

A more discursive approach to some of the ethical issues is to be found in

FINE, S. (1990) *Social Marketing*, Allyn & Bacon.

The following book looks at some of the practical and managerial issues involved in marketing in local government in Britain.

WALSH, K. (1989) *Marketing in Local Government*, Longman.

With regard to market research, the following texts are useful.

MOSER, C. and KALTON, G. (1972) *Survey Methods in Social Investigation*, Heineman (the classic text).

OPPENHEIM, A. (1992) *Questionnaire Design Interviewing and Attitude Measurement*, Pinter.

BRADBURN, N. and SUDMAN, S. (1988) *Polls and Surveys*, Jossey Bass (on public opinion polls).

FINK, A. and KOSEKOFF, J. (1985) *How to Conduct Surveys*, Sage (excellent text for beginners).

Chapter Six:
Developing new services

This chapter is about developing new services in the public sector. This is usually called 'innovation'. The chapter is intended to help you to understand what is involved in innovation, how it might relate to your own organization, and the basic principles of managing innovation. By the end of the Chapter, you should have

- a clear understanding of why/when innovation is necessary;
- a full grasp of the implications for your own organization;
- more confidence to approach the management of innovation.

Like many other management tasks, the management of innovation cannot be approached in isolation. As was seen in the last chapter (Chapter 5), marketing may well play an important role in the initial development of a new service, and the management of change within your organization (covered in Chapter 12) will be the key to its successful implementation.

Understanding innovation

What is innovation?

The best place to start is with your own experience.

Write down examples of the development of new services within your own organization, and then list any features common to these developments which you can identify, and which we might call innovation.

Your examples may have been quite similar or varied. Here are just a few examples of the types of development that you might have included:

1. the computerization of a library catalogue;
2. the setting up of a toy library to provide a resource service to young adults with special needs;
3. the introduction of a neighbourhood watch scheme into an area by the police;
4. training in job interview skills in the sixth form of a comprehensive school;
5. the development of a needle exchange scheme by a health authority in an area of high AIDS risk to young people misusing drugs.

All of these developments involve change — so is all change innovation? The answer to this is 'no'. It is true that all innovation does involve change, but change can occur without innovation. A Housing Department might change its opening hours, for example, but this is hardly an innovation.

If all change is not innovation, then what is it? Have a look again at the common features that you identified. They probably included some of the following four features. First, innovation represents *newness*. Sometimes this can be an absolute form of newness, in the sense of the first application of an idea. Such uniqueness is rare nowadays, however, and 'newness' usually means the introduction of something new into an organization, service or locality.

The second feature of innovation is its *relationship to invention*. Invention is the actual generating of new ideas or knowledge, whereas innovation is the application or implementation of these new ideas. These two processes are often talked of together, but it is important to differentiate between them, in order to understand their management. We shall return to this later.

The third feature is that innovation is *a process and an outcome*. It is possible to talk of innovation as the process of developing new services and also as the actual new service produced by this process. Again it is important to be clear which you are talking about.

Finally, to return to our starting point, all innovation involves *change*. This can mean the transformation of a new idea into a service, the change this imposes upon the host organization, or the way that individual needs are changed by the new service.

Why is innovation important in the public sector?

Such a question would rarely be asked in the private sector, where innovation is seen as an essential part of profit generation. It is the way in which a firm gets a competitive advantage over its competitors. This point is well made by the management 'guru' Peter Drucker (1985):

> Entrepreneurs innovate. Innovation is the specific instrument of entrepreneurship. It is the craft that endows resources with a capacity to create wealth.

In the public sector, however, the issue of innovation is more complex. For a start, public agencies, and voluntary organizations, do not exist to make a profit. Although recent government legislation has introduced an element of competition and contracting into the production of public services, there is still not the same profit motive as the rationale of public sector organizations. Any surplus that they might accrue is not distributed to shareholders, for example, but must be ploughed back into the organization.

The lack of this profit motivation to innovate in the public sector has led some critics of it to argue that it is inherently conservative and bureaucratic and should be replaced entirely by the market. Whilst it is true that the reasons for, and processes of, innovation may be different in the public sector, it is not true that innovation does not take place — as your own examples from your own organization will probably have shown.

Broadly there are two reasons why a public sector organization might innovate. The first is often known as 'top down' innovation. This is where a public sector body needs to rationalize its service provision, as a result of the resource constraints upon the public sector. This often involves meeting an already recognized need more efficiently, perhaps by targeting existing services more accurately, or by developing new cost-efficient forms of service.

Examples of such innovations might be:
- changing the role of home care assistants for elderly people, to focus upon simple nursing care of very frail and vulnerable people;
- introducing smaller buses onto a bus route which could run at a lower cost, but more regularly than larger buses.

The second reason is called 'bottom up' innovation. This involves a social or demographic change leading to pressure for a new form of service in a locality. This is often led by 'front-line' workers, and can cause problems for the organization as a whole, because it is 'ad hoc' and hard to integrate into the existing service provision. However, it is explicitly based upon meeting expressed needs in a new way. It thus expands service coverage, and often effectiveness, with service provision, but at the cost of efficiency to the service as a whole.

Examples of such innovation might be:
- community nurses and social workers agreeing to do joint assessments of people with mental health problems, to decide upon the proper balance of services between the agencies;
- a 'ring and ride' bus service upon a particular housing estate.

These two are different types of innovation, and require different skills from you as a manager.

Think about your own services and try and make a list of the different skills each would require, then compare them to the ones below. See if you can think of any additional ones, and add them to these lists.

Top down innovation	**Bottom up innovation**
Negotiation with other service providers	Awareness of changing needs in your locality
Cost-efficiency/cost benefit analysis	Devolving responsibility to your staff to develop new services
Management of impact of the development upon your staff	Protection of your staff against organizational pressures for uniformity
Promotion/explanation of the development to the local community	Securing appropriate finance for the development
Dealing with conflict from staff/service users as a result of the innovation	Integrating diverse developments into the existing system

Types of innovation

Often 'innovation' is discussed in a way which suggests that it is a unified entity. Yet as our preceding discussion has shown, this is far from being the case. Five types of innovation are frequently talked of. As each is introduced, try to think of an example from your own agency. It is also important to remember that one development might include several different types of innovation in its subcomponents.

'Knowledge push' versus 'need pull' innovation

In this case, innovation is differentiated according to whether it is the result of new knowledge or research, or of new demands arising in the community. It is commonly used in the private sector where it is called 'technology push versus market pull'. This approach is useful in emphasizing that there are two sources of innovation. Frequently in the public sector, though, new services develop from a combination of both these pressures. The provision of community-based group housing for adults with learning difficulties is an example, both because of increased professional awareness of the desirability of such an approach and because of demands from service users and their families to live a more normal life outside of large institutions.

'Distress' and 'slack' innovation

Another approach is to classify innovation depending upon whether it comes about because an organization has to change to avoid extinction (distress innovation) or because an organization is thriving, and so has resources to devote to new developments (slack innovation). An example of the former could be a library department changing the opening hours of its branches onto a rota basis, and sharing staff, to avoid having to close one or more branches down altogether. An example of the latter could be a counselling service introducing group therapy sessions to cope with the number of would-be clients on the waiting list.

The users of an innovation

This approach to understanding innovation makes the point that innovation is not a simple process. Often different users of an innovation will perceive different attributes or effects of it. This is important in reminding managers that the usefulness of innovation is not objective. There can be disagreement on the appropriateness and/or effect of an innovation and the managers introducing the development may have to deal with the resulting conflict. So, for example, the introduction of a new assessment system for students on an undergraduate course could be perceived quite differently by tutors, students, administrators, and would-be employers. The overall assessment of this innovation would depend upon the existing balance of power between these stake-holders.

Product and process innovation

This approach is the one most commonly adopted in the private sector. It differentiates between innovations which are a new product or service for the consumer, and those which involve a new process for producing products and services. This approach has the benefit of simplicity, but it has its problems. Even in the private sector, what might be a product innovation for one firm (for example, a new machine) could be a process one for another firm (which uses this machine to change its production process). Moreover in the public sector most of its products are services, which are themselves processes, rather than tangible objects. This distinction is thus often difficult to make. A residential home for elderly people is more than just its buildings. It is also the process of care that goes on within it, and the interpersonal processes that this involves. Innovations in the care of people within this home are hence both product and process innovations.

Service and user innovation

The final way of approaching innovation is probably the most helpful for managers in the public sector. It involves deciding whether the innovation is about developing new forms of service, or about meeting the needs of a new client group (Osborne, 1994). Taking this approach, you can differentiate three types of innovation:

- *total innovation* — where you develop a new service to meet the needs of a new client group for your organization. This is the most challenging form of innovation, as it involves you in managing major changes in your own organization (or sometimes creating a new one) as well as establishing the needs of a new group of service users. An example of this would be the creation of a new part of a community health service, to provide a 'buddy' support service to people with AIDS

- *expansionary innovation* — where you take a service that your organization already provides, but develop it to meet the needs of a new group of clients. This requires you to manage the transformation of an existing service across client boundaries, and to ensure that you are not simply imposing a predetermined service onto an unwilling group of recipients.
An example of this is the way in which the Probation Service has, in recent years, expanded forms of non-custodial service it had developed for juvenile offenders (under sixteen years old) for use with young offenders (over sixteen years old)

- *developmental innovation* — where you develop new forms of a pre-existing service to meet the needs of the existing clients of your agency. This requires the management of the introduction of a new service to the clientele of your agency. (An example of this would be the introduction of the National Curriculum into schools in Britain.)

In summary: in this section, you have been introduced to the concept of innovation, and explored the different reasons for it and forms that it takes. By now you should be clear that there is more than one form of innovation, and that it arises for many reasons. We have ended by emphasizing the links between developments in the services that your agency produces and the potential user group that you service. The second section of this chapter will now go on to look at the management of the development of new services in more detail.

You should end this section by going back to your original list of developments in your organization. See if you can add any more to it, then think about the reasons for these developments, in the light of your reading. Have these different reasons affected the organization of developments, and if so how? Make a list of these differences for use in the next section.

Managing the development of new services

The innovation process

So far this chapter has been dedicated to helping you to understand the range and depth of innovations that your organization might benefit from. It is now time to move on to talk about the details of its management in practice.

Once again, the best place to start is with your own experience. Think about innovations and developments that your organization has been involved in over the last two years. First make a list of all such innovations that you can think of, then pick two or three of them. For each of these try drawing a 'road map' to show all the stages which the development may have gone through. Once you have done this, share it with a manager who was also involved with the innovation and check out your perceptions. If there are any differences, try and find out why this might be so — it could be related to the different roles that you both took in the development, or its differing impacts upon you, or even whether you approved of the innovation or not.

Your 'road map' should have included some or all of the stages identified in the section on 'The stages of innovation' below. Not all these stages will always be necessary, depending upon the size or potential impact of a development, but you should also consider the reasons for excluding a stage (or why your senior managers chose to exclude it), rather than including it. It is also important to remember that the development and introduction of a new service can be a very long process indeed, from it first being thought of, to its actual introduction. In the case of some services it may well be almost ten years from when a project is thought of to its introduction! Of course, not all projects will need as long as this, but do not underestimate the time involved in developing new services.

It may also be that some of the decisions outlined below are being taken not by yourself but by a more senior manager in the organization. Even though you may control these less, it is still important to understand the process of developing new services as a whole.

The stages of innovation

Identifying the need for a new service

The reasons why new services develop can be many and varied. There is no one 'right route'. The important task for you as a manager is to be pro-active in this. As was suggested earlier, the impetus for development is more marked in the private sector, because of its link to profitability. Although, or perhaps because, this spur is not present in the same way in the public sector, many public sector organizations have in the past fallen into the habit of simply repeating the same services over again. Yet for the public services, particularly those human services dealing with personal needs, the nature of the services needed can change quite quickly.

In further education, for example, there was a need for introductory courses on computing in the early and mid-1980s because of the introduction of personal computers into people's lives. These were new and people did not understand them, so the need was to explain what computers were and how they worked. Recently, however, the need for such courses has dropped. Most people now understand what computers are, either from their schooldays, or from the media. The demand is now for courses on the applications of computers, either inside the home or at work. In this simple example, failure to understand the changing need would mean that a college would be less able to attract students, and meet the needs of its local community.

Your role as manager is to monitor the services that your agency provides against the needs of potential and actual service users. This role was developed in more detail in Chapter 5 on marketing. Here it is worth thinking of some of the events that might give rise to the need to develop a new service.

Firstly, a need might be identified as part of an on-going, or one-off, review of your existing services. In the field of community services for adults with learning difficulties, for example, a system of service planning for users of these services called Individual Programme Planning (IPP) is used to identify the personal strengths and needs of service users, and to develop appropriate services. The strength of this approach for the service is that unmet needs can be aggregated to highlight key gaps in service provision.

Service users themselves are also an important source for identifying the need for new services, and one often overlooked in the public sector. All too often in the past public sector organizations have delivered the services that they thought that people wanted, rather than actually asking the users. There is an important role here for market research, and again this is covered in more detail in Chapter 5 on marketing. Managers also need to monitor demographic information on their areas to watch for changing needs, such as changes in the proportions of teenagers, or elderly people, living in their areas.

New staff can bring a fresh perspective onto the existing ways in which services are provided. They may simply bring a fresh pair of eyes onto existing services or they may bring good ideas from elsewhere. Whatever the reason, it is important to encourage new staff to be (positively) critical about the services that your agency provides, and for yourself and your staff not to be overly defensive about existing services.

Finally, legislation itself can require new forms of public service to be developed. The introduction of the Local Government Act in 1988 required local authorities to develop new forms of providing services, through compulsory competitive contracting rather than by providing these services in-house. The Griffiths reforms of community care services had a similar impact upon both the NHS and local authority Social Services Departments.

The key point is to be open to new ideas and approaches, rather than defensive about the status quo.

Generating new ideas for service delivery

Of course, identifying the need for a new service is only the first step. The next stage is to develop (or borrow or modify) ideas for this service. It is important here to learn from research about innovation in organizations. In general there are two important pre-conditions which will aid the development of new ideas inside an organization.

The first is an open and non-directive style of management, which encourages people to think for themselves and to volunteer ideas. As a manager you may be a source for new ideas yourself, but more often than not you will need to rely on other people — so the more responsibility they have for thinking for themselves the more likely they are to come up with ideas. This requires you to:

1. devolve decision-making and planning as much as possible;
2. encourage people to offer suggestions, whether they are good ones or not — fear of rebuff is most likely to prevent people from volunteering in the future;
3. make innovation and development part of the language and culture of your staff.

The second pre-condition is to encourage the 'cross-pollination' of your staff with staff from other agencies, so that they can learn from each other. Also, if you are establishing a project group to develop a service, make its membership as varied as possible (staff, service users, other agencies). The clash of different viewpoints can be the best way to stimulate new perspectives on an issue.

Many of the sources of ideas for service will be the same as those which identified the need — service reviews, service users, and new staff for example. Do not be afraid to cast a wider net than your own locality. Professional groups can often disseminate ideas of best practice, and you yourself can profit by keeping up to date with research and new developments in your field. Even if you do not have time to read large-scale studies, your trade or professional press will usually keep you informed on developments. Lessons from abroad can also be important.

Finally it is important at this stage of generating ideas to be as uncritical as possible. Nothing is more likely to put people off making suggestions than thinking that they will be criticized. Be as open as possible to ideas from any source.

Evaluation of new ideas

Having (we hope) generated a number of ideas for service development, you now need to start imposing some structure on them. The first stage in this is to evaluate the range of ideas against the need that you have identified. This stage may be controlled by your senior managers, but it is important that you contribute to it. A simple approach here is to develop a 'service specification' for the required service, in the same way that you might develop a person specification for recruitment purposes. To develop this specification you will need to decide:

- what are the essential elements that this innovation must contain (there may be legislative requirements, or issues of access if the service is to be the one used by people with a physical disability);
- what are the preferred characteristics of the service, in an ideal world (you may want to prioritize these to assess your ideas against them).

You can then use this specification to form a check-list, against which to evaluate new ideas, though ultimately you will need to make your own decision. Such a list is an aid to decision-making, not a substitute for it.

In developing the specification it is important to consider whether you want to modify and/or add to the existing services of your agency, or to replace them. Modification has often been the preferred option in the public service. It offers continuity of service and easy assimilation within the existing practices of the organization. It also is likely to produce the least disturbance in the staffing patterns of your agency, and provoke the least resistance. However, the danger is that you may end up with an agency which, like Topsy in *Uncle Tom's Cabin*, 'Just grew'd'! That is, it will be an agglomeration of amendments and modifications, but with no real shape to it and with innumerable blocks to efficiency and service effectiveness.

The alternative, of developing a new service actively from first principles, avoids this danger and may well produce a simpler organization, easy to understand and more accessible to the public. However, such an approach will be in itself more threatening to the staff of your agency, who understandably have an investment in the status quo in terms of their own jobs. It is therefore likely to provoke more resistance to change, and require more time for carrying through.

There is no easy answer to this dilemma. Again this decision may be made for you by your senior managers. You will need to make a decision on the basis of how radical is the change to your agency that the new service requires. What is important is that the decision is a considered one, rather than an easy solution opted for out of caution.

The four stages of implementation

The first three stages of this process have been concerned with designing new services. The next four stages are concerned with their implementation. One of the ironies of developing new services is that, whilst the invention stage requires a flexible organization with plenty of communication and devolved decision-making, implementation requires far more purposeful, and often centralized, leadership in order to carry through the innovation against the various organizational, staffing and environmental blocks that it may encounter. This role has sometimes been called that of the 'hero-innovator', though this overglamorizes the role — as well as making assumptions about the gender of such individuals.

A key role at this stage is *resource acquisition*. The previous stages have involved little apart from your time and some effort from those designing new services. At this stage, the key stake-holders in the organization need to be convinced that resources should be committed to the new project. In order to do this you will need to be able to:

— show the need for the new service;
— suggest its potential benefits;
— demonstrate how obstacles will be overcome;
— have a reasonable plan for the implementation process.

It is important at this stage not simply to expect that a good idea will carry the day, by dint of its own intrinsic value. Developing new services is not a rational process but a political one. It requires you to convince the various stake-holders concerned that the development will benefit them.

Once resources have been agreed, it is important to pilot the service in a small area, for example, one office of your agency. The intention here is to highlight possible faults in the initial design of the new service; to assess the requirements of the organization in incorporating the new service (in administration or new skills required); and to gauge the possible response of the staff of the agency to the new service.

It is important not to confuse the pilot stage with implementation proper. It will benefit from the attention and 'specialness' that a pilot project has, which will not be factors in the full-scale implementation of a development. However, it does offer important lessons for the full introduction of the new service.

When you move into planning the full-scale introduction of the new service to the agency as a whole, it is important to have a fully developed implementation plan. This will not deal with all contingencies (nothing will!) but it will at least cover the major ones. The plan needs to consider

- the process of introduction of the service (i.e. phased or immediate introduction), and its links to the existing parts of the agency;
- the resource implications at each stage, and their source (including any necessary staff training and retraining);

- how the new service is to be explained to staff, and their co-operation and goodwill (for example, by identifying the specific benefits that the service will bring, which they themselves can observe);
- what mechanisms are required for staff feedback on the development, and how will they be shown that their feedback is being taken seriously;
- the anticipation of possible problems with the introduction of the service and how these are to be dealt with;
- how the development is to be evaluated and how the lessons learned from the evaluation are to be fed back to improve the service further.

Never forget that the whole purpose of a new service is (should be!) to benefit the clients of your agency. They too need to be involved and informed about the introduction of a new service, and its evaluation.

The final part of the implementation stage is the 'diffusion' of the new service throughout your organization. It is unrealistic to expect that all the staff in the organization will accept an innovation at the same time. This will only happen over a period of time, and as the benefits of the new service are demonstrated in practice (hence the need to set clearly observable goals for the development). It is also important to remember that people's rejection of a development may not be due simply to their initial resistance or stubbornness. They may have some well-founded reasons for their opposition which you should listen to and learn from. All these issues of implementation will be covered in more detail in Chapter 12 on managing change.

Evaluation and review

Although this is the last stage of the process it is essential that it is considered from the outset of the implementation phase, rather than being an add-on at a later stage. The principles involved are covered in detail in Chapter 8 on performance management. It is important to stress here that the evaluation system should

— be simple and easy to use;
— make sense to those carrying out the evaluation;
— be able to demonstrate the impact of the development to the key stake-holders;
— highlight areas for improvement.

It also needs to include both staff and clients of the organization.

Conclusions

An essential point here is that the developmental process needs to be a positive, not a negative one. Successful organizations encourage development and experimentation and do not penalize those responsible for unsuccessful developments. This is often more difficult for a public sector organization, where there are legal requirements of service to the public, and where a service failure can have disastrous consequences. Nonetheless, unless new development is encouraged, any organization will stultify. The important point is to learn from your failures, and use these lessons to stimulate new services.

Finally it is important to remember that the actual experience of innovation may not be as linear or rational as discussed here. It may appear to be cyclical, or to involve unintended detours; it can often seem apparently irrational, especially when confronting the fears of staff about new development. No plan will deal with all these issues, but taking a serious and measured approach to the planning of new services will at least ensure that you are prepared for difficulties as they arise. Perhaps the best motto to adopt in this process is that from the popular comedy series of the 1980s, *The Hitch Hiker's Guide to the Galaxy*: 'Expect the Unexpected'.

References

DRUCKER, P. (1985) *Innovation and Entrepreneurship*, Harper & Row.

OSBORNE, S. P. (1994) *The Once and Future Pioneers? The role of voluntary organizations in innovation in social welfare services*, University of Aston.

Guided Reading

The following is an excellent collection of readings, covering a whole range of issues concerning innovation

MOORE, W. and TUSHMAN, M. (ed.) (1988) *Readings in the Management of Innovation*, Harper Business.

A good overall study of the process of innovation is

RICKARDS, T. (1985) *Stimulating Innovation*, Pinter.

With regard to the public sector, the following two books give a good over-view of the range of innovative practice

BARRITT, A. (1990) *Innovations in Community Care*, PSI.

Local Government Training Board (1991) *Innovations in Services*, LGTB.

Finally, the following explores some of the more managerial issues involved

LOVERIDGE, R. (1992) *Continuity and Change in the NHS*, Routledge.

Part 3: *Delivering Services*

Chapter 7:
Purchase of service contracting

As was detailed in Chapter 1, the last decade has seen a huge upsurge in the use of contracting for services in the public sector. The reasons for this have been varied and can be different depending upon whom you ask. The most common explanations are:
- contracting is a way to reduce the costs of public services, by reducing the size of the public sector and by challenging the vested interests in it, as represented by the unions;
- contracting offers the users of public services more choice and variety in service delivery than the monolithic public services which have developed since the war;
- contracting is a 'back door' way to privatize the public sector, embarked upon for political reasons by the government;
- contracting will improve the performance and quality of public services, by providing for better ways in which to specify and evaluate these services.

Whichever of these you choose will depend upon your own point of view. However, it is important to realize that there are a variety of rationales behind the move to contract out of public services and, importantly, that you cannot necessarily achieve all these objectives at the same time. Thus, for example, contracting may be able to reduce the costs of public services or increase choices and/or quality, but it may not be able to do all these at the same time. It is therefore important for managers in the public service to be clear about the objectives of their agency, as this will affect the planning of their services.

By the end of this chapter you should:
- Understand what is special about contracting and what it means for purchasers and providers
- have an overview of the key stages and processes in contracting
- have thought about some of the management issues that contracting raises for your agency for you as a manager and for your service users.

Think about your own organization and ask yourself the following questions:
- *Is your organization already involved in contracting out? If so, what do your senior managers want to achieve through contracting (it may not necessarily be clear what this is, and this is important in itself). If not, why is this and how likely is it to happen in the near future?*

- *If you are already involved in contracting, what services has your organization contracted out, or taken on as a contracts for another organization?*

If possible, discuss your answers with colleagues and see if their perceptions are different. If they are explore the reasons for this difference.

It is important to realize that, although contracting has increased over the last decade, it is not a new activity for the public sector. It has been used in varying forms for a long time.

Examples include:

- franchising of bus services (before deregulation);
- laundry services in a Health Authority;
- contracting out of road-laying;
- individual 'out of authority' placements by Social Services Departments for adults and children with special needs, for which there was no relevant resource in their authority;
- purchasing of supplies (stationery, food, etc.) for public organizations.

The two major differences in the present situation are that, first, contracting is now expected not to supplement or extend public sector provision, but to replace it (as with local authority housing). Secondly, it is being extended into service areas where it has not been present before, or where piecemeal contracting is being replaced by contracting for whole services — social and clinical health services are a particularly good example of the latter area.

Because of this it is important for managers in organizations working with contracts to keep two apparently contradictory principles in mind. First, it is important to avoid re-inventing the wheel. Where your agency has experience of contracting services, even in a field unrelated to your own, it is important to learn from this experience. Secondly, it is important to remember the particular nature of your service. Contracting services for vulnerable elderly people is not the same as contracting a road-sweeping service. Different forms of contract and contractual arrangements will be needed.

The purpose of this chapter is not to provide its readers with a manual on contracting. These are available elsewhere, and examples are listed at the end of this chapter. Rather, it is to provide an introduction to the issues that contracting raises for service managers, whether as purchasers or as providers of services.

What is a contract?

In common usage, this may seem to be a nonsensical question. Surely it is an agreement between two people (or parties), or more, to do something. In common usage, this may be so, but in fact how you define a contract will depend upon your point of view. The best starting place is for you to write down your own definition of a contract.

Your definition may have included one or more of the following elements:

1. *A legally binding agreement between two or more parties to do something*
    This is the lawyers' definition, and may seem the simplest. However, the fact that some lawyers make not inconsiderable earnings from 'tort' (contract law) may suggest that it is not quite as simple as it seems. A verbal agreement over a handshake, with witnesses, may well be as legally binding as a multipage legal document duly witnessed.

2. *A means by which one party in the contract agrees to supply a product/service for a third party at a specified price*
    This is a definition more commonly used by accountants. Again, it seems straightforward, but it too contains difficulties. In accounting terms, the specific nature of the sale is important. An agreement by one agency to fund a post in another agency may not be a contractual arrangement, for example, unless it is tied to a specific output or sale of that agency (such as to provide a detached youth service to young people in a designated geographic area), by the second organization. Rather it would be a more general grant to support the youth work of the agency, without specific remit. The nature of the agreement could affect the way in which the accounts of an organization are set out.

3. *A way of reducing the costs of a public sector, by reducing bureaucracy*
    This is a common perception, if not definition, of a contract in relation to the public sector. In fact, however, contracts have their own costs and bureaucracy. In some circumstances, it may well be more expensive to contract out a service than for one agency to provide it itself — particularly where the service is complex and the conditions surrounding it are uncertain. There is a whole branch of economics (called 'transactional economics') which is devoted to the analysis of these transaction costs.

4. *A way of increasing choice for the user of public services, by increasing the number of providers*
    This is a loose definition often used by politicians to justify contracting. Yet contracting, by itself, may not introduce choice. It will depend upon how much competition the market can stand, and upon how easy it is for other suppliers to enter the market. If this requires a heavy investment, an organization, once awarded a contract, may be able to ward off other competitors because of the cost advantage it has, from the investment that it has already made in the service. Moreover, an organization may chose to contract out its entire service to another agency, for financial reasons. In this case there is no increase in choice, but rather the replacement of one monopolistic supplier by another.

5. *A way to ensure accountability by the funders of public services*
    It is often asserted that contracting increases accountability because it requires greater specification of what is required. However, sometimes this is very hard to do or measure, as will become clear in the chapters on performance and quality management, below (Chapters 8 and 9).

Clearly, contracting is no simple thing! For managers the best approach to defining a contract is possibly to be as inclusive as possible. In this book, a contract will be defined in broadly legal terms as 'An agreement between two (or more) parties to provide a product or service to a greater or lesser degree of specificity'.

This definition does not create a deliberate cut-off point between grants and contracts, and indeed it is more of a continuum than a discrete break. There are grants which have many of the characteristics of formal contracts (in terms of monitoring) and contracts which are grants (because of their generalist nature). The important point is that public services are to be provided by a 'third party' upon behalf of the public agency, to their users.

It is also important to realize that there is no one entity as a 'contract' or 'contracting'. Rather it is a cluster of procedures and relationships. Which one is best suited to your purpose depends upon the needs it is to serve.

Important concepts in contracting

Firstly, who are the parties to the contract? Broadly there are two parties. These are the 'client' (i.e. the organization or person that is contracting out the service) and the 'contractor' (the organization or person that is supplying the service). Sometimes these parties are also called the 'purchaser' and the 'provider', or the 'principal' and the 'agent' respectively. An important point for public service managers is where service users come into the contract. They are usually thought of as the client of a service, but unless they are made a party to the actual contract (which could be impractical with some services, such as health care) they are not the client — even though they may still be the user! This raises important issues about how to ensure accountability of a contracted-out service to the users, as well as to the client agency. You may want to think about your own agency, and the extent to which it tackles this issue. Then consider how it might be improved, or initiated if not already done.

Secondly, how are contracts awarded? Again there are two main processes. One is 'negotiated contracting' where the client organization invites one or more contractors to 'tender' (that is, to bid to provide goods or service) for a contract. A decision on the award of the contract is then made on conditions decided by the client, but usually on 'non-price' grounds such as quality or choice.

The second process is 'competitive contracting', where typically the client advertises a tender, usually in the press, and any contractor who meets the service specification (in terms of experience and skills) is able to tender. This is then usually decided upon straight economic grounds of the cost comparisons between the tenders in relation to the full service specification.

Which process your own agency is able to participate in will depend upon which part of the public sector it is working in. For some parts, especially in local government, the Local Government Act 1988 requires that services are put out to compulsory competitive tender (or CCT). Other parts of the public sector, especially in the field of social care, are free to decide how to proceed and here negotiated tendering is frequently used. This is also the case between District Health Authorities and hospitals which have gained 'trust' status under the NHS and Community Care Act.

Thirdly, how are contracts monitored and evaluated? One of the main reasons put forward for contracts, as discussed earlier, is to reduce the cost of public services and/or improve their performance. This is not as easy as it sounds, however. The client of a contract is dependent upon the contractor for the information about the performance of the contract and clearly the contractor has an interest in portraying their performance in the best possible light. This problem is often called the 'principal–agent' problem in economics. In order to solve it through the contract above, the client either has to be highly specific about the service required (which can be very costly in preparing and monitoring the contract) or try to set out a contract which pays the contractor on the basis of performance alone (called 'performance contracting', such as paying teachers on the basis of their examination results, as experimented with in America).

Contracts are therefore no easy solution to improving service quality and effectiveness. Indeed they may raise as many problems for the client organization as they solve, whilst the contractors may be faced with apparently increasingly complex and inflexible contracts to manage. This makes the important point that contracting is no substitute for the management of public services. It is simply a different way to manage them. They require as much management of interpersonal relationships as do direct services. The contract provides the framework for a relationship, but unless the clients wish to spend most of their time in litigation in courts (which is expensive and time-consuming), the relationship needs managing as much as might any other staff that a manager is responsible for. This is most clearly the case in relational contracts, discussed below in the section on 'Contractual relationships'.

Take a service that you are at present responsible for, and look at the way in which it is contracted at present, or how it might be in the future. Ask yourself:

1. *what would be the best way to tender this service, and why;*
2. *how, and to what extent, it is possible to divide your service up into different components to put out to tender, or whether the service as a whole would have to be contracted out;*
3. *who should be party to the contract and how is accountability to service users to be ensured;*
4. *how is the contract to be monitored and evaluated, and in what ways might performance be improved without resorting to the courts?*

With regard to the last part of the exercise you might wish to include such possibilities as

— *training courses*
— *penalty clauses*
— *performance contracts and bonuses*

— *review processes and targets*
— *user feedback processes.*

Pricing a contract

One of the most difficult parts of contracting is deciding how much a service costs. Do you just include the direct costs, such as staff, or other indirect costs, such as the central services of a local authority; what about capital depreciation; and what about such costs as staff training?

The answers to these questions will largely depend upon whether you are a potential purchaser or provider of a service. Depending upon which you are, you will have a vested interest either in minimizing these costs (for a purchaser), or maximizing how much of them you are able to include (for a provider). In simple terms you should expect to include four elements in costing any service. It would be helpful for you to take your own service and try and price these elements yourself, highlighting any area of difficulty for discussion with your senior manager. It could also be instructive to think about how a purchaser and provider might approach their costing in different ways, and what effect this would have.

(a) Direct costs of the service
(b) Indirect costs of the service
(c) Overhead costs
(d) Capital Costs

These financial issues are covered in more detail in Chapter 10 on finance, so they will not be discussed in detail here. However, it is important to recognize three important issues:

- the more specific a contract is, in terms of the actual inputs of a service, the less freedom the contractors will have on how they manage the service. Not only is this demotivating, it may also reduce their flexibility in improving and developing a service.
- public services, by their nature, are often harder to define than manufactured goods. The inputs are more varied, and variable. A stage before actual contracting, therefore, may be to decide which inputs you are going to cost and in what way. You then need to gather information on this basis over a period of time. This will give you more confidence in your pricing policy in the future.
- typically unit costs (the average cost of a unit of service) are used in pricing services, but this is by no means the only, or best, approach. Marginal cost (the cost of producing one more unit of service) may well be more helpful to both purchaser and provider. Moreover, it will probably also be worth considering what economists called the 'opportunity costs' of a service — that is, by deciding to pursue one option, which other ones are you forgoing? Again these issues are explored in more detail in Chapter 10.

Contractual relationships

There are three types of classified relationships, as detailed in Table 7.1. Which type you choose will depend upon the service that you are contracting, the time period involved and your own needs. Classical contracts are useful for 'hard' services, such as catering, which do not require ongoing relationships and where cost savings are important (CCT is a good example of this). Neo-classical contracts are useful for

Table 7.1: *Contractual relationships*

Contractual relationship	Characteristics	Advantages	Disadvantages
(1) Classical	Specific contract between parties for good/services at a certain price	Simple; does not require ongoing relationship; encourages competition	Cannot cope with changing circumstances; requires frequent renegotiation
(2) Neo-classical	Contract between parties for good/service, with facility for renegotiation, either by the parties to the contract, or by resort to a third party arbitration	Possesses some flexibility; assumes a level of trust because of acceptance of need for renegotiation	Is more complex than classical contract, and hence more costly
(3) Relational	Contract is between parties to come together to provide a service, but details of services/cost, decided within the contract	Very flexible in changing circumstances; can cope with complex services; maximizes trust	Is a long-term arrangement and hard to dissolve; precludes competition

Source: adapted from Osborne S. P. (1993) *The Governance of Public-Private Relationships*, Aston University.

providing parts of a service, where circumstances are likely to change, and where there is a level of trust. A voluntary organization contracting with a local authority to provide a nursery with a joint management team would be a good example of this (service level agreements are another example of this type of contract).

Finally relational contracting is a good model for a whole service where the key issues are continuity and trust, rather than competition. A good example of this is where Health Authorities and Social Services Departments have pooled resources within an independent trust, in order to provide mental health services in an area. Here the contract (the trust agreement) provides the framework, whilst the management of the contract is within the relationship. Elements of relational contracting have also been used in America, where 'partnering agreements' have been used, for example, in bridge construction on public highways. The previous experience of such contracts in America was precisely one of delay, cost over-run and extensive (mutual) litigation. Partnering was seen as a mutually beneficial alternative to this, where the client and constructor come together, agreeing problem-solving procedures and mechanisms as part of the contract, and sharing any risks.

What types of contract does your agency work with? Are they most appropriate to your service, or would other ones be more suitable? Can you suggest ways in which the type of contract might be improved? If your agency does not use contracts, then consider what type might be the most appropriate and why.

Types of contract

Having decided upon the type of relationship that you want, you will need to decide upon the type of contract to employ. For relational contracts, this is essentially a document establishing the trust. For classical and neo-classical contracts, however, there are an enormous variety of types of contractual arrangements. The ones below are only the most common. Again, find out which your agency uses or is involved with, and why.

Grant

This is the simplest form of contract, where a sum of money is paid for the general support and the work of another agency. The only requirement is usually for the presentation of audited accounts. For many years this was the form of arrangement used by central and local government with voluntary organizations.

Contracting out

This is where the whole, or part, of a service is contracted to another agency with level of service or and/or cost of the service specified. It is most easy to use with 'hard' services, such as refuse collection, but has also been used for 'soft' services, such as residential care for elderly people. Usually the contract is for a part/whole of the entire service. The most common forms of this type of contract are:

- *block contracts,* purchasing access to a resource, rather than a defined number of uses. They will specify the quantity/quality of *inputs* rather than *outputs*. Because the client is not paying by volume, they will tend to try to maximize the use of the service. By contrast the contractor will take this potential maximization principle into account in their pricing. With a block contract, the client has a stable service, though at an inflexible price, whilst the contractor has a guaranteed income but uncertainty over the level of demand and complexity of the needs of the users.
- *price by case contracts,* here a price is quoted for each individual user/unit of provision. These are usually very detailed contracts and hence expensive to negotiate. If the price is competitive, clients will be able to purchase a quantity of a service at a quality they want. However, if the contract does not specify the volume of users to be served, then the client will face uncertainty as to the size and scope of the service. Similarly for contractors, price by case contract allows flexibility in the volume of users they serve, but does not provide any guaranteed income. This flexibility for both parties to the contract is gained at the sacrifice of a guaranteed service/income.
- *spot purchasing,* where a client can make an individual transaction to take advantage of a competitive market (rather in the way that you might purchase a good at a supermarket, to take advantage of a sale price, or a 'price war' between two competing supermarkets). This can offer good cost saving to the client agency, but makes planning for the service as a whole very hard.
- *costed volume contracts,* which specify a volume of a service and its total cost. Here the client has a guaranteed service for a specified number of users at an agreed price, but faces problems if the demand for the service exceeds the supply that they have negotiated. By contrast the contractor has a guaranteed income, but no control over the complexity of user needs that they will be dealing with.

No one type of such contracts is right or wrong. It depends upon the needs of your agency and your users.

Franchising

This implies a far more long-term relationship between client and contractor. The franchise can be one of the following two types:

- an ownership franchise (where the client contracts out a total unit or service to the franchisee, who provides all the buildings and resources to run the service — as is the case of the franchising of commercial television stations in the UK); or
- an operating franchise (where the client contracts out the management of a service, including the employment and management of staff, but retains

ownership of the buildings and other capital equipment — as has been the case with many local authority leisure centres in the UK).

Franchises are more long-term arrangements than the contracts previously discussed, and imply a degree of dependency of the two parties on the contract. They therefore provide more stability and, potentially, trust in a service, though at the cost of the loss of the market stimulus to cost efficiency. They are most commonly associated with the neo-classical contractual relationship detailed in Table 7.1.

Trusts

These are the most complex form of contract, where two parties join their resources together to form a third party to provide a service (you might want to review an earlier discussion of relational contracts, here). This type of contract is relatively impervious to the market and hard to dissolve, but it is able to deal with complex demands and shifting needs.

The contracting process

Before embarking upon this stage take a service that your own organization has either already contracted out to another party, or taken on as a contract for someone else. If you are not yet involved in contracting, then consider the possible process for a service that you provide at present. Discover for yourself the stages involved (or those that might be involved), then compare them with the ones below.

Not all contracts will go through the same process or processes. It will depend upon the type of contract, whether it is negotiated or competitively tendered for, and upon the relationship intended. However some or all of the following stages will be applicable.

Pre-tender

If this stage is included, it is usually intended to narrow down a wide range of potential bidders to a contract to a shorter 'approved' list. A client might ask contractors to submit for approval in general (by demonstrating financial soundness, a track record of successful service delivery, etc.). Alternatively, this stage might be in relation to a specific form of service, such as refuse collection, and the would-be-contractors would then have to demonstrate experience in that field of work. This stage will also involve drawing up the service specification and the tender documents for the next stage.

Tendering

The mechanics of this stage will depend upon whether a contract is to be decided competitively or by negotiation. If the former, then it will be advertized in the press usually, or to the approved list, if this approach has been used. Bidders will be invited to submit tenders in sealed packages by a certain date, upon the basis of the information given. Where competitive tendering is required by the Local Government Act 1988 then specific criteria apply to the process, which are laid out in the Act.

If the process is to be negotiated, on the other hand, then the client will usually invite one or more potential contractors to submit a tender, with more negotiation about what this tender should involve and the criteria for evaluating it.

Contract award

Again, this stage will often vary depending upon whether the process is competitive or negotiated. In the competitive modes, the tenders will be compared against each other, on a set of standard criteria, and the contract awarded to the bidder who best meets these criteria — usually involving the price of the contract. By contrast, negotiated contracting will involve, not surprisingly, more negotiation concerning the content of the bids and their evaluation against a wider range of criteria than just price. At this stage, contracts may be awarded on the basis of the written bids alone, though it is more usual for the bidders to have to make a presentation to the client.

Contract management

Once awarded, the respective roles of the parties to a contract conform to the 'principal–agent' model described earlier. The role of the client, or principal, is to monitor and evaluate the performance of the contract against the agreed criteria. The ways that this might be done are described more fully in Chapter 8 on performance management. However the client will now have little direct contact with the users of a service. The agent needs to ensure that their service meets the contract specification and is more *directly* concerned with the needs and views of the service users. As well as the performance of the service in relation to the contract, the contractor will therefore also be concerned with its quality, as perceived by service users.

Contract termination/renegotiation

At the end of a contract, there are two possibilities. In the competitive model, the contract will be put out again for tender and the existing contractor will need to bid again — rather like in the franchise tendering process for the commercial television channels in the early 1990s. Although the existing contractor will have an advantage here, because of their knowledge of the market and also the extent to which they have purchased expensive capital equipment, this does not always ensure success.

Alternatively, if the contract was a negotiated one, the client may choose to tender the whole service once more or to renegotiate the existing contract with the existing contractor. This reduces competition but increases service continuity.

At the end of the section on 'Contractual relationships' you were asked to look at the actual or potential process for your own agency. You will probably have identified many of these stages, but may well have found other ones, or variations. This is not unusual. As discussed earlier, contracting is a framework *for management, not an* alternative *to it. Its precise nature will depend upon the requirements of your service.*

It is important that you review the contracting process in the light of the needs of your service, whether as a purchaser or a provider of services:

— *is the most appropriate process being used?*
— *can you recommend any modifications to the process?*
— *what is the impact upon the users of the service?*

Conclusions

This chapter has introduced you to some of the complexities of contracts and to some of the differing ways to look at both contracts and contracting. The important part is always to remember what the purpose of the contract is, so that contract management does not become an end in itself, and remember also that contracting is not an alternative to managing a service, but supplies a different framework within which to do it. The precise form/type/skills involved will depend both upon the public service involved and upon the purpose of the contract.

References

OSBORNE, S. P. (1993) *The Governance of Public-Private Relationships*, Aston University

Guided Reading

There is a great deal of literature covering this area. A general discussion of the issues confronting service providers is found in

GUTCH, R. (1990) *Partners or Agents?*, NCVO.

Two other books give practice based discussions of the issues confronting both purchasers and providers

Brook, R. (1989) *Managing the Enabling Authority*, Longman.

LOHMANN, R. (1991) *Managing Contractual Services in the Non Profit Agency*, Temple University Press.

The following two books are concerned more with specific examples of, respectively, different forms of contractual documents and different forms of contractual services

Davies, A. and Edwards, K. (1990) *Twelve Charity Contracts*, NCVO.

DEMONE, H. and GIBELMAN, M. (ed.) (1989) *Services for Sale*, Rutgers University Press.

The following two books are more specific guides to the contractual process

KETTNER, P. and MARTIN, L. (1987) *Purchase of Service Contracting*, Sage.

SOLACE (1988) *Managing Competition*, HMSO.

Finally the following book looks at the important issue of how to cost services

CALLAGHAN, J. (1992) *Costing for Contracts*, Directory for Social Change.

Chapter 8:
Performance management

This chapter is intended to help you to understand why and how to measure performance in your organization. It starts off by discussing what is meant by performance, and how it is measured, and then goes on to explore how you might do it within your organization. By the end of this chapter, you should:

- understand why performance management is important to public sector organizations;
- understand the problems and pitfalls involved in performance management;
- have thought about how to develop performance management systems in your own organization.

Background to performance management

Although public sector organizations have always had to account for their performance in some way, it is only since the early years of the Conservative government of the 1980s that this has become a key requirement of public sector management. In performance management now there are three central thrusts:

- a concern for 'value for money' (VFM) in all evaluation processes;
- a concentration upon what are known as the 'three Es' (economy, efficiency, effectiveness);
- a focus upon 'management' rather than 'administration' as the task of managerial staff in public sector organizations.

These issues were covered in more depth in Chapter 1, and you may want to refer back to it now.

Because of the complexity of the task of performance management in multi-objective programmes or organizations, such as public sector organizations, the 'rational' model of decision-making (March, 1990) is often employed in performance management. This concentrates upon breaking down the decision-making process into simpler stages and linked sub-sets of decisions. It assumes that decisions are made inside organizations in a linear fashion and on the basis of available information. Performance management has often been seen as an important component of this rational approach in the public sector. It is important for you to realize that this model is not accepted by everyone. In particular it has been criticized for:

- not realizing the political dimension of performance management, and how it might be used by political groups or parties for their own ends (such as demonstrating the success of a programme that they were responsible for);
- not accepting that the information available for any one project or programme is only partial, and so any evaluation will, at best, be only partial;
- not acknowledging that performance management is itself a political exercise. What comes out of any evaluation will very much depend upon who is conducting it and their point of view (just think for a moment how different the evaluation of your service might be if conducted by yourself, or your senior manager, or a user of the service).

It is important for you to recognize these limitations upon rationalist performance management. However, it remains the dominant model and the one within which you will need to work. The rest of this chapter is committed to helping you understand this model and use it to best effect.

The building blocks of performance management

As was said above, the key to performance management in the rationalist model is the ability to break down the service process into a number of blocks. The model employed here is of this process as a system (this idea was introduced in Chapter 1) the key components of which are:

— inputs,
— outputs,
— outcomes.

INPUTS are the things that go into making up your service. These can again be divided into two types:

1. **substantive inputs**, such as staff time, capital equipment, and the running costs (power, etc.) of a service,
2. **quasi inputs**, such as the characteristics of a building a service is in (is it old and adapted or purpose-built) and the personal characteristics of your staff and clients.

Whilst it is possible to quantify the former, and put a financial value upon them, this is much harder, if not impossible, to do with quasi-inputs, though their effect upon a service must also be acknowledged.

OUTPUTS are the services and activities that your organization produces, using the inputs at its disposal. These inputs undergo a transformation in the service process, which combines them in different ways to produce outputs. Examples of outputs are:

1. the number of hours that a teacher spends in front of their class;
2. the number of places available in a day centre for elderly people;
3. the number of arrests that a police officer makes on their shift.

OUTCOMES are the hardest component of the service process to measure. They are the impact and effect of a service upon its recipients. These can be divided into the:

1. *intermediate outcomes* of a service for its users, known as its impact example, the extent to which a reminiscence therapy group helps an elderly people improve their short-term memory);
2. *final outcomes* of a service for its users, known as its effect (for example, the extent to which the therapy group mentioned above led to an increase in self-esteem for an elderly person, because of improved social functioning).

Outcomes are notoriously difficult to measure, which is why they are often ignored in performance management systems, but they are very important. Put bluntly, they are the ultimate test of whether your organization is achieving its goals.

These 'building blocks' are all brought together in Figure 8.1. It is important to remember, as this figure shows, that public services do not exist in a vacuum. They exist and are influenced by their social environment and their communities. This is why the 'same' service in two different communities will have quite different characteristics — it is responding to its particular community. Indeed if it did not do this it would be accused, quite rightly, of being inflexible and not responding to local needs.

It is also important to remember that the environment will affect the outcomes of a service for its users. The impact, and effect, of the probation service upon a young offender will be influenced strongly by the peer group of that young person. In designing performance management systems, it is therefore important to remember the limitations of a service, as well as its potential, so that you do not indulge in unrealistic expectations for it.

Figure 8.1: *'Building Blocks' of initial and final outcomes*

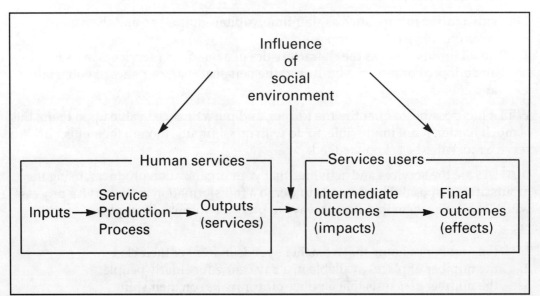

Take your own service and write down the inputs, outputs and outcomes of it, as you see them. You should also specify the key factors in your local environment which affect that service. If possible discuss these with a colleague and your line manager. Do they have a different perspective? If so what is it, and why might this be so? Remember that your perspective upon performance depends upon your position in the process. Keep these lists for use later in the chapter.

Performance management

What is performance management

Performance management is the evaluative process by which a view is reached about the performance of a set of activities measured against the achievement of specified objectives. A number of separate elements can be contained within it:

- **Performance appraisal** — the prior assessment of the degree to which proposed activities are likely to achieve their objectives, and the formulation of indicators and targets by which the performance of the activity or programme can be monitored and evaluated in the future (not to be confused with the appraisal of staff performance, as part of the personnel systems of an organization).
- **Performance monitoring** — the ongoing assessment of a programme, in terms of both its objectives and its process, often concentrating on the evaluation of the achievement of 'lower level' objectives, such as physical progress, meeting of deadlines and the keeping within budget guide-lines.
- **Performance (ex-post) evaluation** — the retrospective evaluation of a programme against its objectives.
- **Performance indicators** — surrogates for the levels of performance. Often quantifiable indicators are utilized because of their ease of use, but qualitative indicators are also used, and are (at least!) equally important and harder to interpret.
- **Performance management** — the overall process of ensuring that:
  - performance assessment is an integral part of any programme from its outset;
  - it is understandable to those gathering the data and to those analysing and using it;
  - the results of performance assessment are used to inform all levels of programme planning and implementation;
  - the performance assessment process is oriented toward enabling performance improvement.

Why assess performance?

Clearly, performance management should not be viewed as an end in itself or a sole determinant of future change; this would belie the complexity of public services. Rather it is a particular way of gathering and reporting information in order to alert managers to any potential problems or benefits from possible changes. It is also a way to ensure accountability for the use of public money by both public and voluntary organizations. This is a difficult task and requires a sophisticated approach by both public sector agencies and voluntary organizations.

What are the components of a good performance management system?

- performance assessment needs to be an integral part of any programme or organization, bringing benefit to all concerned. It is feasible to impose it from top down, but then its reliability and impact are limited. Staff are unlikely to collect (or to collect accurately) information that they do not understand, or see no use for (even if it is useful to other levels of management);
- indicators need to be set and agreed in a way which is understandable to all. It is no use designing a sophisticated set of indicators which defy staff attempts to implement them;
- performance assessment needs to concentrate on strengths and positive outcomes as well as organizational weaknesses and shortfalls. If the evaluative process is perceived as too negative then, rightly or wrongly, staff will often find ways to sabotage it;
- performance assessment has a cost in terms of time and money. The cost of more elaborate and sophisticated systems needs to be measured against their potential gains and a balance should be struck;
- performance assessment needs to be judged by the extent to which it has enabled performance improvement. This must be kept firmly to the fore in designing the performance assessment system.

Putting together a performance management system

What are you trying to achieve?

The first stage of this is being clear about the goals of a service. It is hard to measure the performance of a service, particularly its outcomes, if you do not know what it is trying to achieve! It is important, therefore, to agree clear, and achievable, objectives for your unit or section of your agency.

You may also want to set a performance 'target', based upon this objective, which is what you hope to achieve over the next year. This is usually couched in terms of the outputs of a service, but it could also indicate its outcomes.

Thus, for example, the objective of a Fire Service might be to reduce the number of fires occurring in its neighbourhood, and to minimize the loss of life and property through any fires that do occur. A performance target for the coming year could be to reduce the outbreak of fires caused by electrical faults, through a public awareness campaign, by 5 per cent.

How are you going to measure performance?

The usual way to do this is through the use of performance indicators. These are immensely useful as checks upon your performance, but remember that they are only indicators, they are not the service itself. Some common examples of performance indicators are to be found in Table 8.1, and are considered further in the next section.

Table 8.1: *Examples of common performance indicators*

Quantitative	
Unit cost	Total cost of services divided by number of places provided in service
Overhead/output ratio	Total administrative and central office costs divided by costs of actual activities and projects
Occupancy rate	Optimum use divided by actual use
Take-up ratio	Number of users from target group using a service divided by total size of target group
Throughput ratio	Number of people actually using a service in a given time period divided by optimum usage rate of a service in a given time period
Qualitative	
Complaints analysis	Analysis of content of complaints about a service in a given time period
Satisfaction levels	Immediate reactions of services users to it
Case reviews	Analysis/judgment of extent to which a service has met the identified needs of individual users
Exception reporting	Highlighting and analysis of cases where a service fails to achieve a specified target

Figure 8.2 illustrates a way of thinking about the possible indicators that you might want to use. You should consider how these different types of indicators relate to the 'systems' model of a service introduced in Figure 8.1. Ideally you should try to ensure that you develop indicators of the inputs, outputs, and outcomes of your service. Which ones you chose will depend upon the nature of your service. Ideally, you should use a mix of all four types of indicators, as they are illuminating different things about the service. It is also important to involve your service users in the process of defining performance indicators. After all, they are in the best position to gauge the performance of a service.

Figure 8.2: *Performance indicators*

	Using easily available material	
Quantitative indicators	Output indicators (e.g. beds per 1,000 population in a residential home)	User perceptions of services (e.g. feedback boxes)
		Qualitative indicators
	Target take-up (proportion of the target group for a service that uses it)	Longer-term outcomes (effects) for clients (using structured interviews to assess effects)
	Using information that is more difficult to collect	

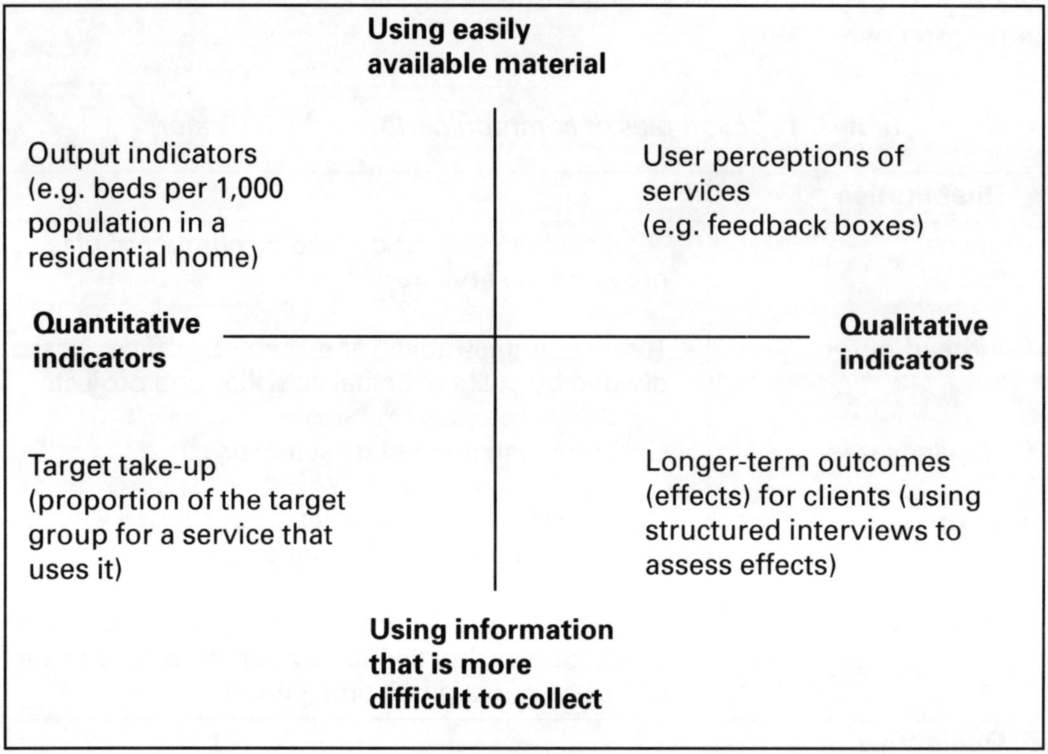

Now take some time to do one of the following exercises.

Either *Take the existing performance indicators for your organization and examine what they are trying to measure. Is the information they require easily available? How are they interpreted and used? Who chooses them? Now try and improve them. If they are taken from just one or two of the quadrants in Figure 8.2, then try and develop indicators from the other quadrants. Discuss with your line manager how you might use these new indicators.*

or *If you have no performance management system at present, then begin to design one for your unit of service. Do not be over-ambitious. Be clear about the objectives of your service as a whole and then set performance targets for it, based upon the inputs, outputs, and outcomes of your unit of service. Then try to set a performance indicator for each quadrant of Figure 8.2 for each of these targets. This will help you measure your performance in achieving this target. Now discuss the possibility of implementing this performance management system with your line manager.*

Note: *Do not forget the lists of the inputs, outputs and outcomes of your service that you made at the start of this chapter. These should help you in designing your indicators.*

Performance indicators and value for money

Traditionally, there are three different conceptual levels of performance at which indicators are directed, in order to evaluate a programme. It is important to remember that indicators are only the tools for managing performance and not targets, or ends in themselves. These levels are:

— economy,
— efficiency,
— effectiveness.

However, it is also important to consider 'equity' in public programmes, for the sorts of reasons we discussed in the section on 'The value base of the public sector' in Chapter 2.

Measurement of **economy** is required to ensure that for any given cost level, inputs are maximized. It requires performance indicators which relate to input objectives. Typical indicators could include:

- comparisons of staff wage levels (for given qualifications and experience) across regions, divisions, agencies, etc. and over time;
- comparisons of purchase costs of materials and other inputs (of given quality specification) across regions, divisions, agencies, etc. and over time.

Measurement of **efficiency** is required in order to ensure either that, for any given level of output, required inputs are minimized or that, for any given level of inputs, output is maximized. Typical measures of **efficiency** include, for any given level of inputs:

- the levels of service provided;
- the levels of activities carried out;
- the numbers of outputs produced;
- the unit costs of a service.

The measurement of **effectiveness** is undoubtedly the most challenging to undertake. This covers both the political and strategic decisions about which potential groups of users should be targeted for services; and the management and operational decisions affecting the impact of services upon the welfare of the agreed target population. The reaching of these initial decisions is a crucial stage in linking the overall objectives of an organization to the target population which it is seeking to service. It is no use trying to provide the 'right' service to the 'wrong' target group. The process of market segmentation talked about in Chapter 5 is important here.

Two categories of performance indicators are used most frequently to assess effectiveness. They are targeting and impact. Examples of these kinds of indicators are:

- targeting
  — target group users as a proportion of all users;
  — target group users as a proportion of total target population.

- impact
  — changes in user well-being;
  — changes in user welfare;
  — user satisfaction;
  — achievement of agreed policy goals;
  — longevity of 'community' organizations created.

Measurement of **equity** is required to ensure that the distribution of outputs is consistent with the policy of the government with regard to the distribution or redistribution of resources and services to the population as a whole. This requires assessing the degree to which a service provided is fairly distributed and accessible to the individuals/groups for whom it is intended. It may include:

- the geographical distribution of users;
- the distribution of users across client groups;
- the knowledge of availability of service within client groups;
- the accessibility of service to potential users (for example, wheel-chair access for people with disabilities).

The relationships between these four different types of performance indicators and the different parts of the service production progress are illustrated in Figure 8.3.

Figure 8.3: *Performance indicators used to indicate the level of achievement at different parts of the service production process*

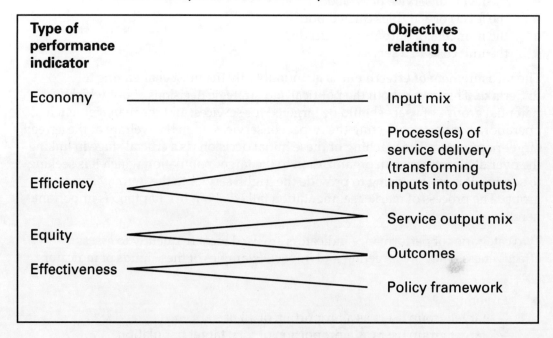

At which organizational level should performance be assessed, by whom, and how often?

Because of the complexity of public organizations and programmes, performance must be assessed at multiple levels within them. This is because the purposes, and information requirements, of each level are different, if interconnected. These levels thus require measurement of different things. At each level the information gathered is expected to be useful both to those gathering it and to those above them. In most cases, it is also expected that an organization will need to assess performance at three levels:

- **project or team level** — performance assessment needs to be able to help project team managers and staff with the progress of their own objectives and motivate them to solve problems. This might be at the level of the performance of either individual staff members, or of the team as a whole.

Performance information also needs to be in a form which can be aggregated to the:

- **programme or departmental level** — performance assessment needs to be able to help programme/departmental managers to utilize their resources appropriately and to ensure that their projects and teams are working to the priorities of the organization, and to help them with medium-term decisions about resource acquisition and allocation.

This information also needs to be in a form that can be aggregated to the:

- **strategic level** — performance assessment needs to enable senior managers to ensure that the different components of the programme/organization adhere to its overall aim and strategic plan, and to make medium- to long-term decisions about resource acquisition and allocation.

You need to be clear at which level you are operating, as this will affect the construction of your performance management system. However, you also need to be aware of the needs and purposes of other levels of your organization. Chapter 11, on 'Making information work for you', will consider how the information needs of different levels of an organization can differ, and will help you further in considering this issue.

The differing dimensions of performance management

Having discussed the practicalities of performance assessment, it is also important to understand that it can cover a number of different dimensions of the work of an organization. There are six dimensions which it is most important for you, as a manager in the public sector, to concentrate upon:

- **Context monitoring** involves examining the extent to which the impacts which the programme or organization is seeking to achieve are also being influenced by the activities of complementary or competing agencies, and by changing socio-economic and institutional circumstances.

- **Strategy monitoring** involves checking on a regular basis that the activities carried out and the overall level of inputs and activities comply with the strategy, and specifically with its objectives, targets and priorities. This is a basic need for any organization to ensure compliance with its strategy and resource allocation.
- **Progress monitoring** involves checking that programme targets are being met on time. This is particularly important to maximize the use of resources, to control overspending and prevent underspending, and to highlight problems as they arise. It is particularly critical in large programmes or organizations, where there tends to be 'over-programming' at the beginning of each financial year to allow for the likely slippage of projects and where there needs to be an early identification of slippage so that, if necessary, projects which can start quickly can be brought forward from the next programme year. Whilst financial control information is the commonest form of progress monitoring, physical progress on capital projects and achievement of tasks by key dates can be at least as important.
- **Activity monitoring** involves a more detailed monitoring of activities and numbers of projects and tasks in progress. It is the basis for efficiency reviews, and particularly for comparisons of unit costs and productivity. It requires frequent recording but less frequent reporting and analysis than in the case of progress monitoring.
- **Impact monitoring** involves assessing the achievement of the highest levels of objectives, normally in terms of the impacts (outcomes) achieved on the targeted client population of organizations. It is difficult and therefore generally occurs less frequently, though conversely it is one of the most significant forms of performance assessment.
- **Catalytic monitoring** involves assessing the effect of a programme or organization in influencing other important and influential organizations and individuals in the provision of a service or the meeting of a strategic objective. It is required to assess the wider impact of the programme/organization in meeting its key objectives.

All of these dimensions of performance management may not be required, necessarily, for your unit of service. However you should always decide whether or not they are needed, rather than simply assume that they are not. Some final examples of the different types of performance indicators that you could use for these levels are included in Figure 8.4. This is taken from a performance management system that one of the authors was involved in designing for the Rural Development Commission (PSMRC, 1991).

Go back to your Performance Management System that you designed earlier. Have you taken all of these dimensions into account in it? If not, consider how you might evaluate your performance in the missing dimensions, and try to build them into your system. Again, discuss the practicalities of this with your line manager.

Figure 8.4: *Performance monitoring*

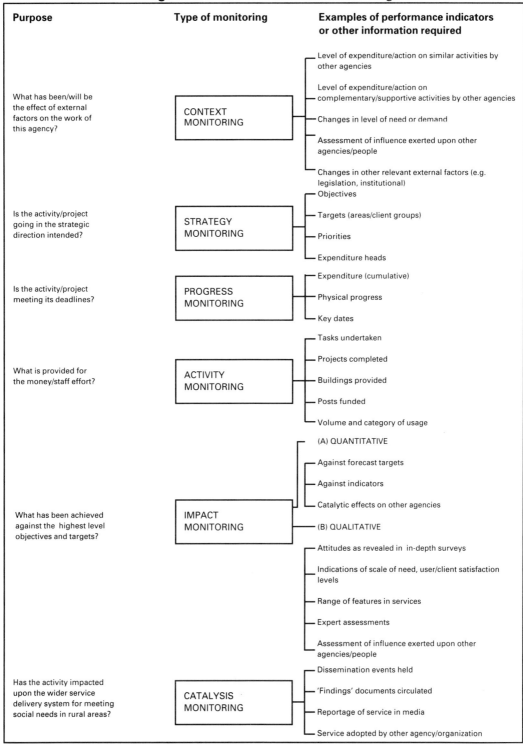

Source: Public Sector Management Research Centre (1991), *Managing Social and Community Services in Rural Areas*, Aston University.

Conclusions

This chapter has taken you through the issues involved in designing performance management systems. In conclusion, it is important to remember the principles of good performance management detailed earlier (in the section 'What are the components of a good performance management system?'), and also the three key limitations upon any system:

- performance management has a cost. You need to balance its sophistication against its cost;
- the system needs to be easy to use and interpret for staff and clients, or it will not be implemented;
- performance management is a tool for your organization and its clients, not an end in itself. It has to be directly related to the purposes of your organization and the needs of your clients, or it will become a sterile, irrelevant exercise;
- performance indicators are of limited, or no, use by themselves. They are only tools for you to use. They provide you with the information with which you can make your judgments about the performance of your service against, for example, the targets/plans of your organization; your service standards; your past (and future) performance; and other organizations with whom you may be working (or competing) in a service.

References

MARCH, J. (1990) *Decisions and Organizations*, Blackwell.

PUBLIC SECTOR MANAGEMENT RESEARCH CENTRE (1991) *Managing Social and Community Development Programmes in Rural Areas*, Aston University.

Guided reading

AUSTIN, M. (1986) *Evaluating your Agency's Programmes*, Sage (A good no-nonsense guide to evaluation).

DAY, C. (1989) *Taking Action with Indicators*, HMSO (A thorough guide to the use of Performance Indicators, particularly quantitative ones).

DAY, P. and KLEIN, R. (1990) *Inspecting the Inspectorates*, Joseph Rowntree Foundation (A research study of the work of Inspectorates in the human services).

LAWRIE, A. (1992) *Quality of Service. Measuring Performance for Voluntary Organizations*, NCVO (A beginners guide, for those in the voluntary sector).

Chapter 9:
Ensuring quality of service

This chapters seeks to help readers answer four questions:
- What is quality?
- Why is it important?
- How do you measure quality?
- How do you design systems to ensure that the services that you produce are of a high quality?

By the end of it, you should be clear about the nature of quality, how you might define it in relation to your own agency, and ways in which you might go about ensuring/measuring it.

What is quality?

The first thing to understand about 'quality' is that it is not a thing but a concept; a way of thinking about things. It is not possible to see or touch quality, and different people will often disagree about how much 'quality' a particular product or service possesses. Despite its elusive nature, quality is nonetheless crucially important for the public sector. Whilst performance management is about the use of resources by an organization in achieving its goals, 'quality' represents an assessment of a service by its consumers.

Before going any further, you should attempt to define 'quality'. What are its key components? If you would find it more easy, you can define it in terms of your own service. Write down your definition.

You may have had difficulty in specifying the nature of 'quality', and found that you were trying to cover both the process and the content of your service. In general, quality covers both these components of a service, and so can be defined in two ways. The first of these is what is called 'fitness for purpose' (FFP). To the industrial producer the measurement of this is relatively straightforward, usually by reference to the appropriate British Standard. This will specify the characteristics of a 'quality' product in an objective, if arbitrarily defined, manner. Thus, if a car engine part is not to within, say, 1/100 centimetre of the required standard, it is of poor quality, because the machine that it is intended for will not tolerate the divergence. That is, the component is not 'fit for its purpose'.

With manufactured products, FFP is relatively easy to define. This is not so in the public sector, however, where the outputs of public sector organizations are usually services and are usually related to individually defined (i.e. subjective) needs. Try and define the FFP of the following services:

— the casualty ward of your General Hospital;
— the Drug Squad of your local police force;
— a Sixth Form College;
— a Social Education Centre for adults with learning disabilities.

You may have found the first two quite easy. The purpose of a casualty ward is to provide emergency medical treatment, so its FFP relates to the extent to which it achieves this. Your local Drug Squad is required primarily to prevent the use of illegal drugs. This requires it both to discourage use, by education, and to reduce it, by catching users, and especially suppliers, of illegal drugs.

The other two examples are more complex. With regard to the Sixth Form College, what exactly is its purpose? It is no use simply saying 'to provide an education', as this can be interpreted in different ways. Does this mean to prepare for public examinations, to get the best possible academic potential out of any individual, or to provide a social education for him/her? It might legitimately be held to include all three; if so, the question is what is to be the balance between them.

With the Social Education Centre, there is also a question of who is its prime 'customer'. Is it the adults who attend to learn a range of practical and social skills, or is it their carers, who are able to have a break from their care whilst knowing that their charges are in a safe place? Depending on your answer, this could mean providing different services in order for the Centre to be 'fit for its purpose'.

FFP, then, is not straightforward, but it is very important. Before you can start deciding how far your service is fit for its purpose, you need to define clearly what its purpose is. Following the example below, you should specify what your service is and what its purpose(s) is(are), in the left-hand column. If necessary put these purposes in order of importance. (In doing this exercise, you might find it useful to refer to the work that you did on your own organization, in Chapter 5, 'Marketing public services'.) In the right-hand column, you should write down how you might ascertain that your service has fulfilled its purpose—that is, is 'fit for its purpose'.

Example: Day Centre for Elderly People

Purpose of service	*Example of FFP*
To relieve isolation and to provide companionship which encourages social interaction	Range of social activities to meet different needs
To provide stimulation to meet different needs	Range of practical and intellectual activities provided

To provide relief for carers of an elderly person	Carers have regular breaks of sufficient length to help them 'recharge'
To prevent the need for elderly people to enter institutional care because of any of the above factors	Service allows elderly people who would otherwise receive institutional care to remain in their own homes (defined as percentage of the potential client group)

The second definition of quality is not to do with the purpose of a service, but with the process of its delivery. This is even more subjective than FFP might be, because it needs the evaluation of the subjective experience of a service by its users. It is better to think of this characteristic of quality as having to do with its 'excellence in experience' (EIE). To take an easy example, if you eat in a restaurant, no matter how good the quality of the food is (how 'fit for its purpose' it is), you might define the meal as a bad experience, because of the rude and poor service that you received.

In terms of services, it is helpful to think about what Normann (1991) calls the 'moment of truth';

> perceived quality is realized at the moment of truth, when the service provider and the service customer confront one another in the arena. At that moment they are very much on their own. What happens then can no longer be influenced by the [organization]

The 'moment of truth' (and its EIE) of a public service can result from many factors, depending upon what the service is. Draw up your own list of factors which could affect your own service, then compare it to the one below. If you have included any factors not listed here, consider if they are specific to your service or might be found elsewhere.

— Staff attitudes to their own roles and to their service users
— Furnishings/decoration of buildings
— State of buildings
— Discrimination
— Explanation offered as to necessity of a service
— Waiting times for services
— Reception upon arrival
— Punctuality

With regard to public services, both these characteristics of quality are important. A service must both be fit for its purpose, in the sense of addressing identified needs (such as a home care service which is focused upon completing those tasks which enable elderly people to continue living in their own homes), and offer an excellent experience (in the aforementioned home care service, by ensuring not only that identified tasks are completed, but also that the service is provided in a friendly and companionable manner, and on time).

Finally in this section, having separated out the two components of quality, you should then bring them together, to provide a definition of a 'quality service' for your agency. Write it down, as you will need to refer to it later in this chapter.

Why is quality important?

The easy answer would be that good professional practice in public services requires it. Unfortunately such good intentions have frequently not been able to produce good quality public services, over the past two decades. The reasons for this are debatable and range from criticism of the professional and 'expert' nature of many public services (the 'we know best' syndrome of professionals) to condemnation of the overarching financial framework. In 1986, for example, the Audit Commission condemned the 'perverse incentive' to private residential care that the Social Security system provided, in contradiction to the expressed policy of the Department of Health, of 'community care'.

Within both the Health and Social Services, the Conservative government of the 1980s identified the corporate structure of these agencies as responsible for the poor quality of their services. Because both the Health Service and Social Services Departments were responsible for the planning and provision of their services, little incentive, it was claimed, existed to improve their quality. Indeed, in the times of economic stringency, there was a constant pressure to reduce costs. The prevailing reality was characterized by the Griffiths Report (1988) as one of service managers filling existing services to capacity, irrespective of the service quality, in order to reduce unit costs.

For many public services, this has resulted in an encouragement or requirement to split the planning and financing (or purchasing) of services from their provision, in order to create a market for the services (this was discussed in more detail in Chapter 1, 5 and 7). Quality is important to public sector managers involved in both these functions. For the purchasers of services, they need to be satisfied that a service will meet the needs for which it is being purchased; failure to do so will leave the service users, upon whose behalf they act, unhappy with their service. For the providers of services, quality is even more important. If a service does not provide good quality for its users, then it is unlikely to survive. Existing and potential service users will, if alternatives are available, go elsewhere.

Of course, if it were simply (!) a question of quality, then the task might be less daunting for public sector managers. However, there is the additional complication of the costs and budget of a service. The question that public sector managers may have to ask is therefore not 'what quality of service should I be providing' but 'what quality of service should I be providing within my budget'. Purchasers of services will need to balance quality against cost in comparing tenders, whilst service providers will need to decide what their users are prepared to pay for, in terms of quality, and what they will not pay for.

Why evaluate quality?

Turning to the question why it is necessary to evaluate quality, a cynic, or ardent libertarian, might argue that there is no need to evaluate quality, as the market will always be its final arbiter. Whether this is true or not, such a terminal evaluation is of no use to the service provider, who requires to be one step ahead of the market. It is of no use for service managers to contemplate the lack of quality of their service once it has closed down, when ongoing quality evaluation could have enabled them to change the service and avoid the ultimate sanction of the market.

At a societal level, it is also undesirable to let the market be the sole arbiter of quality for public service. One of the distinguishing features of a service is that consumption occurs at the same time as production, with the consumer as an active, not passive, participant. Within a school for example, education is not produced in one room by teachers and then passed on to their students in another room. The two processes happen together and are as influenced by the characteristics of the students, as by those of the subject under study or the teacher.

Because of this, there is a social cost to letting the market decide on the quality of public services, as its users may become commodities. In the above example, the students face being shifted from school to school, which itself has a personal and financial cost, as the market decides which school will survive and which will not. If one wishes to avoid this, it is necessary to develop systems to evaluate quality, which will allow service producers to respond to shifting needs, rather than always having to close.

How to measure quality

Having decided that it is important for managers of public services to evaluate their quality, it is necessary to move on to the key issue of how to do it.

To start with, you should consider your own agency:

1. *does it have systems to evaluate quality, and what are they;*
2. *do they cover the characteristics of both fitness for purpose and excellence identified earlier;*
3. *how are the results of these systems used.*

A common problem with evaluating quality, especially in human services, is the confusion over what is being measured — in particular whether it is the quality of service that is being evaluated, or the quality of life of its recipients. These concepts are not identical yet can be confused in practice. Thus, for example, it is possible for adults with learning disabilities to receive a poor quality residential service, but to have a considerably higher quality of life because of their involvement in an excellent day occupation service. Similarly someone having a brain tumour removed may ultimately have a higher quality of life, because of the operation, but receive a poor quality of service because of the poor nursing cover on the ward.

Despite these problems, quality of life has nevertheless often been used as a way of evaluating the quality of a service. There are many good reasons not to do this. First, 'quality of life' is a complex subject, yet quite simple measures have often been used to try and evaluate it. In residential care of the elderly, for example, eye contact with other people has been used as a measure of the quality of life of an individual, yet this can be affected by a number of factors, such as short-sightedness or life habits, which make it hard to generalize in such a way. Secondly, the supposed links between quality of life and quality of service are not made explicit. It is not sufficient merely to assert these links, they need to be demonstrated. Without this, one is left with the problem of whether a change in the quality of life was brought about by a change in the quality of a service, or by other factors. It is not possible to prove that those succeeding in their chosen careers, did so because of their school education, though many school teachers would like to think (or hope) so.

Thirdly, the relationship between quality of life and quality of service may not be a constant one and may change over time. It can be misleading to measure over too short a time-scale. Recipients of a hip operation could have a significantly lowered quality of life in the months immediately following an operation, for example, because of the limited mobility and discomfort that they experience. In the longer term, however, their quality of life would be significantly enhanced by their increased mobility.

Another example of this is a day service for adults with learning disabilities. A prime objective of this service could be to raise the expectations of its users as to achieving their potential in life. Success in this could lead to a short-term lowering of personal satisfaction as service users strived, unsuccessfully, to fulfil their newly realized potential, but to a raising of it in the longer term. In both these cases, a good quality service could be indicated by a lowering of the perceived quality of life of its recipients in the short term, in the expectation of an increased quality of life in the future.

Fourthly, many evaluation tools have often been developed within research contexts. They are often time-consuming to administer and may require expert skills to carry out. Even if they represent the most sophisticated developments in evaluation, their cost (in time and money) could outweigh their potential benefits.

Fifthly, many measures of quality rely upon its definition by 'experts', rather than by service users. Critics have for a long time argued that not only does this devalue the experience of the service users themselves (Ackoff, 1976) but it also reinforces their dependency upon external definitions of what makes a good service, rather than their own observations. In this respect, best business practice in the service industries is in advance of its public sector counterpart, in the development of a user-based approached to quality (Hensel, 1990).

Finally, and perhaps most importantly, many of these quality evaluation systems are not integral to the service production process, being only 'add-ons'. Because of this they are frequently experienced as an unnecessary intrusion by staff and consumers alike.

To summarize, many of the existing approaches to the evaluation of the quality of a service based upon the quality of life of its recipients are problematic. They often only give a partial view of this quality of life, the links between quality of life and quality of service are often not made explicit, the procedure itself is complex and time-consuming, and is not seen as a proper part of the service delivery process. The readers should review the quality evaluation systems of their own organizations and examine whether they suffer from any of these problems. If this turns out to be the case, they should ask themselves how the problem(s) might be resolved.

The most obvious approach is to steer clear of the issue of quality of life entirely, and to concentrate upon quality of service. It is what the service manager can influence most directly. A framework for considering quality of service is shown in Figure 9.1, taken from the work of the Social Services Inspectorate (1990), on developing quality standards for the residential care of elderly people.

Think about your own service in terms of this framework. It may well help you separate out the different components of your service, and the relationship between them. Once you have done this then draw your own version of the framework, and keep it for future reference.

This framework is useful when supplemented by the work of Ackoff mentioned earlier. He argues for service provision to be treated as a system, rather than as a series of separate problem-solving exercises. Thus, the key managerial role is not individual decision-making, but management of the system as a whole. We shall return to this later in the chapter.

Within this system, Ackoff argues, quality is best evaluated not by external experts with proxy measures, but by the direct participation of the service user. This participation will not only give the best evaluation of the quality of service, but will also in itself contribute to this quality. Once again, think about your own service. If consumers are involved in its evaluation, is it a genuine exercise, or just a cosmetic one? How might their involvement be improved? If they are not involved, how might you go about involving them, what obstacles to this might you face, and how might you overcome them?

Designing a quality evaluation system

Following on from the above point about a public service being a system, it is now time to examine the implications of this for measuring quality, and designing a quality evaluation package for your agency.

The first stage in doing this is to get a clear view of your own service as a system. To do this, it is useful to use the model of a service developed in the previous chapter on performance management (Chapter 8). This specified the relationships between the inputs, outputs and outcomes of a service, and the influence of the social environment upon these. In Chapter 8 these different parts of the service delivery process were analyzed in terms of their impact upon the performance of the service. Here it is intended to examine their influence upon the quality of that service. In

Figure 9.1: *Framework for considering quality of service*

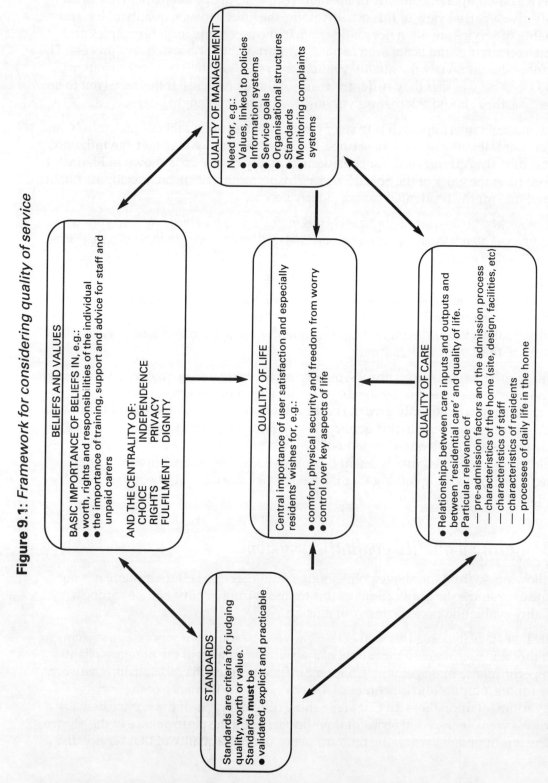

Source: Adapted from Social Services Inspectorate (1990) *Guidance on Standards for Residential Homes for Elderly People*, HMSO.

practice, of course, both of these are interlinked, so that quality and performance management systems often go hand in hand. It will be useful for you to remind yourself of how you analysed your own service using this model. Figure 9.2 (page 142) will take this model a stage further by linking the service components to the quality of service and quality of life.

This systems approach to quality evaluation has three benefits. First, it breaks down the service system into meaningful 'chunks' and allows differential analysis of them (for example between intermediate and final outcomes). Secondly, it gets away from the tendency to define quality in terms of the types of indicators one is using (for example quality of life becoming defined as the amount of eye contact between the residents of a home for elderly people, as discussed previously, rather than being one proxy by which to measure the actual quality of life). Rather, attention is focused upon the relational issue of the connections between different service components.

Finally, the framework does allow for evaluation of the effect of different levels and types of inputs and outputs upon quality of service and quality of life. As such, it clearly has potential for linking the issue of quality to resource allocation.

The second stage is to establish some clear rules for quality evaluation.

You should again reflect upon your own agency and its quality evaluation systems. Think about their strengths and weaknesses and then draw up your own list of 'good practice' principles. If you are able to, discuss these with a colleague and decide how you would modify your existing quality system in order to incorporate your principles of good practice.

Six principles are suggested here, based upon the reading list at the end of this chapter. The overriding theme is that quality evaluation should be an integral and participative part of the service process, not an add-on. These principles are:

1. Any evaluative system must be an integral part of human service provision and not either a separate or an additional process.
2. Any evaluative system must fit the purpose for which it is intended and not simply gather that information which is most easily available.
3. Any evaluative system should build upon existing knowledge and skills. It should be simple to use and not require specialists for its implementation.
4. Any evaluative system should actively involve all participants in a service, not solely the management. It must be demonstrably useful to these participants and not be perceived as a bureaucratic process imposed from the top down.
5. Any evaluative system must focus upon how to ensure that services fit the needs of their consumers and not vice versa.
6. Any evaluative system must produce findings which are usable and are used.

Once again, think about the quality system of your agency. Does it satisfy these principles? If not, what would you need to do to modify it to do so?

The third stage of designing a quality management system is deciding when you are going to evaluate quality. Traditionally there are two approaches to this, called quality assurance and quality control. Quality assurance usually occurs before service production, and seeks to develop mechanisms to ensure that good quality services are being produced (examples of quality assurance include charters of the rights of service users, service standards, job-related training packages, and quality circles intended to identify areas of poor service and improve them). Quality control happens during and after the delivery of services. It is about ensuring that they come up to your standards (examples of this include complaints boxes, contract monitoring procedures, and service inspections). Further examples of both quality assurance and quality control systems will be found in the section on guided reading at the end of this chapter.

It is a mistake to counterpoise these two approaches. A good quality evaluation system requires both. Quality assurance allows for the development of good quality services, rather than simply the correction of problems as they occur. Quality control allows you to pick up any problems which do occur, resolve them, and then feed the issue back into the quality assurance system for the future.

Once again, think about your own quality system, and decide what is the balance between these two approaches. Is it the right balance, and are they linked systems? (Because of their interdependence, both these features are often pulled together in 'Total Quality Management', or TQM, systems (Oakland, 1989).)

Thinking of these stages of designing a quality management system as a whole, Figure 9.2 illustrates one way of how they could be applied in practice. This is certainly not the only way that could be proposed, but it is one which attempts to combine ease of use with effective and meaningful evaluation. It comprises a quality assurance stage and two quality control stages, and builds upon existing frameworks and expertise. Again you may want to refer back to your work in Chapter 5, on marketing, as you go through this process.

Stage I is the quality assurance stage. It requires a clear service philosophy and strategy which links the identified needs which the service is addressing to its objectives and outputs (fitness for purpose). This is necessary in order to focus the service upon its targeted area of need. It also requires a clear statement of the value base of the service in terms of both professional values and the centrality of the consumer. This is important in order to contribute to an organizational culture which positively promotes a responsive and participative service production process (excellence).

Both of these need to be stated in a way which can allow their translation into objectives capable of being monitored in service production. An example of this is the way that the so-called 'five accomplishments' (community presence, choice, competence, respect, community participation) can be used to evaluate the achievement of the service philosophy of normalization for people with learning disabilities. An alternative approach is that of the 'hierarchy of objectives' (Mallinson and Bovaird, 1988). Whichever approach is chosen, the philosophy and objectives of a service will need to be reviewed regularly, in the light of the feedback from the quality control stages.

Stage II is the first quality control stage. It is concerned with the process of service provision and service outputs. It requires service managers to be informed about the local demography and pattern of potential consumers. This information can then be used to assess both the efficiency of the service in reaching its target population and in providing the services it requires, and the extent to which that target population is covered. In this way, service outputs can be related to consumer needs (fitness for purpose). It also requires the evaluation of the direct experience of the service process by consumers, through an abundance of feedback loops (for example, suggestion boxes, questionnaires, quality circles, informal/formal meetings). No matter how 'effective' a service might be, it will not be experienced by consumers as a quality service if the process is not a good experience (excellence).

Stage III is the second quality control stage. It is concerned with the relationship between service outputs and consumer outcomes, both intermediate and final. Intermediate outcomes need to be evaluated in terms of the relevance of the service (and its outputs) to identified needs, and progress towards meeting them. A potential mechanism to do this exists in the needs-based participative planning systems presently used in services for people with learning disabilities (such as Individual Programme Planning, or Shared Action Planning). Such systems allow both regular (six-monthly) assessment of individual progress toward personal goals, by measuring sub-objectives, and their aggregation for evaluation of the quality of the service as a whole.

Final outcomes require evaluation at longer intervals (say, two-yearly) of success in meeting personal goals. It is a mistake to expect easy mechanical formulae for this process. It requires an integration of professional and service user judgments and the negotiation of conflicts and dissonance. It also needs an understanding of the relationship between the service itself and the social environment which its consumers inhabit. However, it is clearly facilitated by reference to the agreed objectives of the service, and their specification with regard to the needs of individual service users. This emphasizes the point of viewing monitoring and evaluation as an ongoing and integral part of the service process, rather than an add-on, at a later stage (fitness for purpose).

Stage III also requires the periodic evaluation of the well-being of consumers and their life satisfaction in areas relevant to the service. A number of relatively straightforward instruments exist to measure this (for examples see George and Bearon, 1989), which are appropriate for use in human services (excellence).

Taken together, these three stages provide a quality evaluation system which is based upon an understanding of the role and processes of human service production as a system, which is integral to these processes and relevant to consumers, staff, and managers (and builds upon existing knowledge and skills), and which allows for the appropriate evaluation of levels of both quality of service and quality of life. It is illustrated in Figure 9.2.

Figure 9.2: *Quality evaluation cycle*

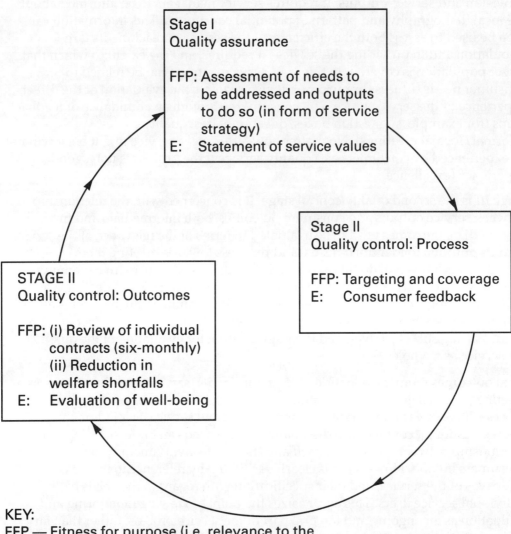

KEY:
FFP — Fitness for purpose (i.e. relevance to the achievement of the objectives of the service)
E — Excellence (i.e. relevance to the experience of the service as a process)

Designing your own quality management system

By now you should have a good understanding of what goes to make a good-quality public service and have thought about the ways in which to evaluate its quality. It is important to remember that there is no such thing as a 'ready-made' quality system which you can plug into any organization. Your quality system needs to be designed with the needs of your service and service users uppermost in your mind.

In order to design your own quality system, you need to go through the following steps which contain some practical suggestions for you to discuss with your colleagues.

The starting point has to be the purpose(s) of your organization; start with the service that you want to provide, and work backwards to where you are now, especially in terms of resources. You may not live up to your expectations (yet!), but you will be clear about where the gaps are, so that you can think about what you need to do to fill them. Go back to your earlier thoughts on the purpose(s) of your organization and the examples of services fit for its purpose. Now think what needs to happen before a service is delivered in order to ensure its 'fitness for purpose'. To take the earlier example of a day centre for elderly people, one of the purposes was to provide companionship and the example of fitness for purpose was to provide a base of social activities to meet different needs. In order to enable this to happen you might want to ask the users of the services what sorts of social groups/activities they would like (market research), rather than choosing on their behalf.

Having established what sort of service you want to provide, you now need to develop quality assurance (QA) mechanisms to ensure that this happens. Ask yourself what you need to do to ensure the type of service that you want to create. Add your requirements to Table 9.1.

Now you need to decide what quality control (QC) mechanisms you are going to use to check on the quality of your services. Remember here that you need to measure both the ongoing process of service delivery and the outcomes for your service users. Remember also that, as with performance management, your mechanisms need to be easily understood by those who use them, be seen to have purpose and produce results which are used, and highlight positive as well as negative aspects of the service.

Finally, you will need a review mechanism for correcting deficiencies in the service noted by your QC system and integrate the lessons learned into your QA system, to prevent the same problem arising again.

Above all, remember to be realistic. It is no use designing a sophisticated quality management system which is beyond the resources or ability of your service to implement. It is far better to start off with limited goals and expand gradually, building upon your success. Your customers and colleagues are more likely to subscribe to a system which has shown its worth, rather than an ambitious plan which is unproven.

Table 9.1: Quality management pro-forma

Purpose of organization:

Example of FFP: Example of EIE:

QA mechanisms required for good quality service:

QC mechanisms required to monitor quality of services:

Review mechanisms:

Conclusions

This chapter began by looking at the nature of quality and its importance in public services. It went on to examine existing mechanisms for evaluating the quality of service on the base of the quality of life of its consumers. It concluded that their discreteness and assumption of causal relationships limited their usefulness, as did their time-scale and cost of implementation. The chapter then went on to propose a framework and guidelines for evaluating quality which clarified the relationships in the service provision process within a systems-based framework. It ended by offering a possible way of applying these in practice.

The conclusions of this chapter are brief. First, the evaluation of the quality of service and quality of life of its consumers is important and needs to be carried out in a way which identifies, rather than obscures, the relationships between the differing components of the process of service provision and consumption and which recognizes it as a system. Secondly, it needs to highlight where quality of service can affect quality of life and where it cannot. Finally, it needs to produce findings which are useful not only to service managers but also to staff and consumers. In a real sense evaluation must not just monitor and measure quality in human services but contribute to it.

References

ACKOFF, R. (1976) 'Does quality of life have to be quantified?' in *Operational Research Quarterly*, (27) pp. 289–303.

AUDIT COMMISSION (1986) *Making a Reality of Community Care*, HMSO.

GRIFFITHS, R. (1988) *Community Care. An Agenda for Action*, HMSO.

HENSEL, J. (1990) 'Service quality improvement and control: a customer based approach' in *Journal of Business Research*, (20) pp. 430–454.

MALLINSON, J. and BOVAIRD, T. (1988) 'Setting objectives and measuring achievements in social care' in *British Journal of Social Work*.

NORMANN, R. (1991) *Service Management*, Wiley.

OAKLAND, J. (1989) *Total Quality Management*, Heinemann.

SOCIAL SERVICES INSPECTORATE (1990) *Guidance on Standards for Residential Homes for Elderly People*, HMSO.

Guided Reading

There are two good texts which discuss some of the conceptual and ethical issues involved in quality manaagement, and which also give good practical examples of quality systems.

BALDWIN, S. *et al.* (ed.) (1989) *Quality of Life*, Routledge.

ROBERTSON, A. and OSBORN, A. (ed.) (1985) *Planning to Care*, Gower.

Two further books give practical examples of quality systems in public services

BESWICK, J. *et al.* (ed.) (1986) *Evaluating Quality of Care*, BIMH.

WARD, L. (ed.) (1986) *Getting Better All the Time?*, Kings Fund.

GRIFFITHS, L. and BEARON, L., *Quality of Life in Older Persons*, Human Sciences Press.

A good source for attitudinal and satisfaction questionnaires in relation to quality of life

Chapter 10:
Managing finance

We mentioned in Chapter 1 some of the ways in which public sector organizations are changing. One area of this change is the devolution of management responsibility to those local units which provide public services directly (e.g. schools, hospital wards and neighbourhood offices). As Chapter 9 (on quality of service) discussed, the managers of these local units not only have to endeavour to provide quality services, but they also have to consider the ways in which these services are resourced. Managers of devolved units may be given detailed budgets stating the amount of money to be spent on each of the categories of salaries, supplies, premises-related costs, etc. They then have to monitor and manage their spending against this budget. Increasingly, however, such managers are only provided with an overall cash limit and they must first plan how to allocate this between the various resource demands and then monitor its consumption.

The devolution of managerial responsibility is increasingly associated with splitting the roles of purchasers and providers, leading to two groups of managers with differing, but complementary financial needs. Purchasers need to be able not only to specify the type, amount and quality of service to be provided, but also to estimate, or make judgments upon other people's estimates of, the cost of providing a service. Providers of service need to be able to estimate such cost when they are asked to bid for a contract to deliver services. They must subsequently translate such a bid into a manageable budget for their service unit. Categorizing someone solely as a purchaser or as a provider may be artificial; as internal trading increases managers are likely to be purchasers of some services and providers of others. For example, a central finance officer will be the purchaser of computer services, but the provider of payroll services.

This chapter takes you through the components of financial management skills and knowledge required in the above situations. Effective financial management has been described as having five key elements (CIPFA, 1991, pp. 7–8):

- **planning**, including setting clear objectives and performance targets;
- **budget setting**, agreeing the level of resources to be used in carrying out the planned activity;
- **activity and expenditure**, including specifying and purchasing services together with direct service provision;

- **budget monitoring and control**, collecting information about actual performance, including costs, and comparing this with the plan or budget. Taking action to keep within budget;
- **review**, re-examining the plan in the light of practical experience to improve the approach for the future.

The chapter first of all considers the issue of managing a budget, it looks at what a budget is and how it can best be managed. It then goes on to consider the planning of budgets and the ways in which the amounts of money allocated in budgets can be estimated and decided. The split between purchasers and providers and the creation of internal markets for services has created a need to develop more sophisticated methods for estimating costs, particularly as the need is to estimate costs not only for a block of service provision, but also for the individual units which make up this block. This is the final concern of this chapter. Whilst working through the chapter you will find it helpful to talk to the budget holders you work with and the accountant responsible for advising managers in your service area. Clearly this chapter can only act as an introduction to these areas. For those who wish to go further, a guide to further reading is provided at the end.

Throughout the chapter you should remember that there is no one right answer to questions like: what does service X cost?, what should be the budget for service X? The answers to these questions depend upon the time-scale involved and the accounting rules which are being applied. Accounting is as much an art as it is a science.

By the end of this chapter you should:

- understand the main components of a budget and the process by which they are constructed
- be able to describe the advantages and disadvantages of devolving budgets
- be clearer about how to manage a budget and the problems which may be encountered
- be clearer about the differing ways in which 'cost' can be defined and what is meant by direct, indirect, fixed and variable costs
- have a basic understanding of the two main approaches to costing: absorption and marginal costing

Managing budgets

It is important to be clear from the outset what we mean by a budget.

What do you understand by the term budget? Write down your definition.

We can define a budget as a plan of action (usually short-term) expressed in financial terms. That is, it is a plan of the financial implications of how we are going to deliver services. Frequently people consider a budget as an allocation of money. However, if we think of our own personal budgets we are concerned with both planning and estimating sources of income, and types of expenditure. Budgets fulfil a number of purposes:

- Planning
  — Translating strategy into operational plans
  — Determining the level of resource required to provide a service
- Co-ordinating — The various activities of the organization
- Controlling
  — Providing a basis for monitoring actual expenditure and income against plans
  — Accountability; making someone responsible for all or part of a budget
  — Authorization; budget approval generally provides authorization for expenditure

In many public sector organizations two sorts of budget are produced according to the type of expenditure being planned:

- Revenue budgets — which focus on revenue expenditure (and its financing); that is, expenditure on day-to-day running costs (such as salaries, heating and stationery)
- Capital budgets — which focus on capital expenditure (and its financing); that is, expenditure on things of lasting value (such as land, buildings and major items of equipment).

The day-to-day concern of most managers is with revenue budgets and this is the focus of this chapter (those interested in capital budgeting should refer to Coombs and Jenkins (1991) in the 'Guided reading' at the end of the chapter).

Traditionally budgets in many public sector organizations have been highly centralized. They were planned centrally, decisions on the level of resources available were made centrally, and decisions on how these resources were to be used were likewise made centrally. In some cases, these decisions were not communicated to front line managers, who had little responsibility for managing their service provision within a given resource level. Their role was to provide a service and they may have only found out about the limits on the resources to provide this service when a moratorium on expenditure was introduced part the way through the year.

The devolution of financial management responsibilities aims to align management and financial responsibilities so that the staff who make service decisions are aware of and responsible for the financial implications of these decisions. In devolving financial management it is important to devise a system where there is only one budget holder (person responsible for a budget area) per budget, in order to avoid confusion and strengthen accountability.

To what extent are budgets devolved in your own organization? Who are the main budget holders and what items of income and expenditure are devolved to them? (If you have difficulty with this question refer to Figure 10.1 which shows the pattern of budgetary devolution within a Further Education College.) If possible set out your answer as in Figure 10.1.

Figure 10.1 *Budgeting structure within a F.E. college*

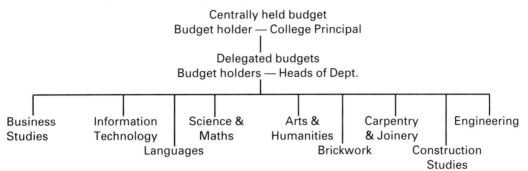

Budget items held centrally

Employees
  Support staff salaries & wages
  Caretakers' salaries & wages
  Administrative & clerical staff salaries & wages

Premises
  Repairs, alterations, maintenance
  Energy costs
  Rents and rates
  Water services
  Fixtures & fittings
  Cleaning & domestic supplies

Transport
  Travel payments } for support
  Car allowances } staff

Supplies & Services
  Marketing
  Professional fees
  Catering service
  Central use of postage & telephones
  Central use of computer

Income
  Grants
  Sales
  Tuition fees
  Other fees & charges

Rationale for items held centrally
All these items of expenditure are negotiated by the Principal and her management team. They commit the expenditure and should therefore be accountable for its control.

All income is at present credited to the central budget. There is some discussion taking place about decentralising certain of the income targets such as tuition fees.

Budget items held by Dept. heads

Employees
  Lecturing staff salaries

Transport
  Travel payments } for lecturing
  Car allowances } staff

Supplies & Services
  Equipment & materials
  Furniture
  Printing & stationery
  Exam fees
  Dept. use of postage & telephones
  Dept. use of computer
  Subsistence & conference expenses

Rationale for items devolved to Depts
With the exception of staff cost all items are directly controllable by departmental heads. Staff costs are controllable in the long run and departmental heads are responsible for 'bidding' for extra staff and are left to determine their part-time requirements, therefore they should be responsible for their control.

Budgets may be devolved in a number of different ways:

1. They may (as in our Further Education College example) be devolved on the basis of the functional divisions within the organization.
2. They may be devolved on the basis of the services delivered (in the Further Education College example, the budget could have been devolved to the various course directors).
3. They could be devolved on the basis of location (for example, if the college were spread over a number of sites, the overall college budget could have been devolved to a head at each of these sites).

Figure 10.2 exemplifies how budgets within the Health Service might be subdivided along these lines.

Figure 10.2: *NHS Budgets subdivided by subjective costs, functional management, management units & specialities (or clinicians)*

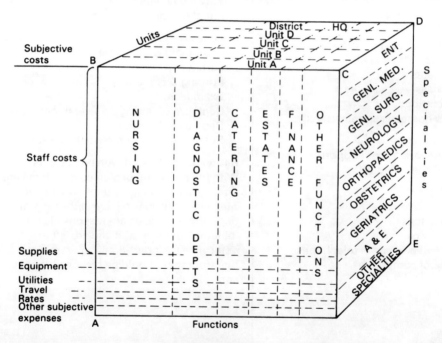

Source: J. Perrin (1988), *Resource Management in the NHS*, Van Nonstrand Reinhold, p. 36.

The potential advantages of budgetary devolution are:

— Quicker/improved decision-making
— Increased flexibility at the local level
— Increased commitment at the local level
— A better use of resources

The possible disadvantages are:

— Discretion at the local level may distort the policies and practices of the service area as a whole
— Financial management responsibilities may reduce the time available for service duties
— A reduction in the flexibility for switching resources at the organizational level

If not necessarily a disadvantage, a concern voiced by organizations considering budgetary devolution is the actual or perceived lack of skills on the part of the potential budget holders.

Let us consider the management of a devolved budget within the context of an example. A district physiotherapist receives a budget statement showing the amount of money available for the different grades of physiotherapist, the amount for medical aids and supplies and the amount for travel (see Figure 10.3).

Figure 10.3: *Physiotherapy budget 199X/199Y*

	£	
Pay (incl. employer costs of NI & superannuation)		
District physiotherapist	19,760	
Seniors (Grade 1)	47,704	
Seniors (Grade 2)	38,498	
Basic	46,996	
Aides	23,323	
Total pay		176,281
Non-pay		
Medical & surgical supplies	3,891	
Travel	1,760	
Total non-pay		5,651
Total budget		181,932

The next logical step is for this physiotherapist to be told that s/he is responsible for delivering services within this budget allocation. To this end, not only is an initial statement of the budget allocated provided, but the manager would then receive regular updated statements (traditionally every month) showing the amount expended to date (see Figure 10.4). The norm would be for this budget to be cash-limited, that is, the total of the budget should not be exceeded, the cost of inflation, pay awards, etc. would already have been estimated and included in the budget figures.

Figure 10.4: *Budgetary control statement for Physiotherapy Budget (Period 6 out of 12)*

Head of Account	Budget for year £	Planned expenditure to date £	Actual expenditure to date £	Variance to date £
Pay				
District Physiotherapist	19,760	9,880	9,880	—
Seniors (Grade 1)	47,704	23,852	23,852	—
Seniors (Grade 2)	38,498	19,249	19,249	—
Basic	46,996	23,498	23,498	—
Aides	23,323	11,662	11,998	−336
Total pay	176,281	88,141	88,477	−336
Non-pay				
Medical & surgical supplies	3,891	3,113	2,998	+115
Travel	1,760	704	1,305	−601
Total non-pay	5,651	3,817	4,303	−486
Total budget	181,932	91,958	92,780	−882

In theory budget management is straightforward; what happens in an organization is an extension of the way in which you would manage your personal or home budget. In order to manage within a budget allocation you need to:

— know what elements of expenditure the allocation is meant to cover
— plan how this expenditure is to be spread over the period of the budget (usually a year)
— monitor actual expenditure against planned expenditure on a regular basis and take corrective action if the two are diverging significantly

In the case of our physiotherapist, the following answers have been arrived at in relation to the above:

● The items of expenditure to be covered by the budget are listed under the headings on the left-hand side of the statement in Figure 10.4. In order to be able to provide a physiotherapy service other forms of expenditure are incurred (e.g. the provision of office space for the physiotherapists, the servicing of this office space with heating, cleaning, telephones, etc.), but for the time being these are not included in the district physiotherapist's budget.
● The planned phasing of the budget allocation over the period of the budget is known as *budget profiling*. The way in which the example budget has been profiled (*see* Figure 10.4) is:

— The salaries of the physiotherapists are evenly spread over the year, so six months into the year it is assumed that half of this budget will have been spent.

- — It is assumed that the majority of medical aids and supplies will be purchased in the first half of the year.
- — Historically the travel budget has been allocated on the basis of 40 per cent for the first six months and 60 per cent for the second six months.

- In monitoring expenditure the budget holder looks at the planned expenditure to date against the actual expenditure to date, the difference being shown in the column headed 'variance'. In our example there is little variance except for travelling expenses. In this case, the budget holder needs to decide whether the initial budget profile is accurate enough. Frequently such profiles are based on the pattern or phasing of expenditure in the previous year. If the budget profile is deemed to be accurate then the budget holder needs to consider how to ensure that future expenditure under this heading does not exceed the total available for the rest of the year. It may be that the workload level was greater than anticipated and this has involved extra travel; in these circumstances it may be possible to obtain additional resources or permission to overspend. The likelihood is, however, that it will be difficult to obtain an addition to the budget, and any permission to overspend will mean carrying over a deficit into the next financial year and hence starting next year with even less money available under this heading. It may be possible to cover overspending on travel by 'viring' (transferring) money from the supplies budget, but this is unlikely to be a long-term solution to the problem.

Whilst budget management in these circumstances is relatively straightforward, there are a number of problems which tend to arise in practice.

Drawing upon your own experience of budget management, what problems might budget holders face in managing their budgets?

The common problems which arise are discussed below.

- The budget holder may not be given details of the budget allocation until after the financial year has begun.
- The allocation may change part of the way through the year, and as expenditure has been planned on the basis of the original allocation it may be difficult to adjust to the new allocation (particularly where it is revised downwards) and still provide the required level of service.
- The budget may not distinguish between (a) items of expenditure and income which are the responsibility of the budget holder and controlled by him or her and (b) expenditure and income over which the budget holder has no control, but which are nevertheless attributed to the budget.
- The common complaint is that the original allocation of funds may in any case be insufficient for the level of service which is expected or demanded. For example, the Disabled Persons Act can lead to assessments of need which a local authority is then required to meet, regardless of whether sufficient resources are available. As we said above, most budgets are cash-limited and

are expressed in out-turn prices, that is, the level of inflation has already been estimated and added in. A common feature of budgetary allocation is the underestimation of inflation. Many would argue that this is a constant feature of central government's public expenditure planning process and this has implications for the level of funds allocated to, say, local government and the NHS.

- The budget holder may not be given the freedom to *vire* funds from one heading to another to accommodate changing circumstances.
- Another common problem is the lack of up-to-date budget monitoring information for the budget holder to work with. These problems fall into a number of categories:
  — Timeliness: the budget monitoring information does not arrive soon enough after the end of the period to which it relates. There are examples of the budget statement for June not arriving until November. The more financial information systems move away from intermittent paper printouts of information to the provision of computer terminal access to the budgetary information systems themselves, the more will this problem disappear.
  — Accuracy: many budget holders complain that they do not believe the figures appearing in the expenditure-to-date column. Much time is spent checking whether things have been incorrectly coded to a particular budget heading, or whether the amount of money itself has been correctly entered. The more remote the coding and entry of information from the service area incurring this expenditure the more likely this is to occur.
  — Relevance: the information provided is not relevant to the needs of the budget holder or is not in a usable format.

Figure 10.5: *Types of accounting system*

Accounting system	Time at which income is recorded	Time at which expenditure is recorded
Receipts and payments (Cash accounting)	Cash received	Cash paid
Income and expenditure (Accrual accounting)	Goods despatched with invoice	Goods received with invoice
Commitment accounting	Order received	Order issued

  — The status of the income and expenditure figures: by this we mean the point at which income is recorded as income and expenditure is recorded as expenditure. There are basically three points at which this can occur and these are referred to as three types of accounting system. Figure 10.5 illustrates this. Clearly a manager whose budget statements are based on cash received and cash paid, needs to be wary of figures relating to expenditure to date, especially where large volumes of supplies are purchased throughout the year. It is for these reasons, as well as because of concerns about accuracy, that many budget holders operate their own parallel budget monitoring systems. Such duplication of tasks is wasteful of resources, but may be considered essential until the budget manager has confidence in the budget monitoring statements produced by a central financial information system.

Estimating costs and planning budgets

Where detailed budgets are not provided for you, or where you are requested to bid for all or part of your resources, you will need to be able to identify and estimate the cost of providing your service. You may also need to estimate the various types of income you might receive. This information will then feed through to your budgetary plan. An example should help to clarify this process.

Our example is the budget for a central training unit within a medium-sized local authority. The training manager has been asked to produce a budget estimate for this unit for the forthcoming year. S/he has little existing budgetary information to draw upon because previously the training unit budget was an indistinguishable part of the overall Personnel Department budget.

How could the Training Manager set about this task? What steps would you take in trying to estimate this budget?

A good starting point would be to identify all the different items of expenditure incurred by the training unit in delivering its services. Such a list might include:

— trainers' salaries
— outside trainers' fees
— the hire of training venues
— stationery and photocopying costs
— travel expenses
— office accommodation costs
— central services charges (e.g. your share of the cost to the finance department of operating the payroll which administers the salaries and wages of your staff)

The next important step would be to find out something about the 'rules of the game'. What types of expenditure are to be included in the Training Manager's budget and what items of expenditure will be borne elsewhere? For example, you can imagine two types of budget: one where only the costs which vary with the amount of training are included (e.g. training room hire, outside trainer fees and travel expenses), and another where all the possible costs associated with training are included (later in this chapter, in the section on 'Costing units of service', we consider how costs can be categorized in terms of direct, indirect, fixed and variable costs).

Having discovered the nature of the items to be covered by the training budget there is then a need to estimate the cost of each of the items included. One important thing to remember about costs is that 'actual cost' is not a simple matter of fact, but an amount of expenditure defined by rules about what is to be included and what is not. In the case of our example, there is the question of whether an estimate for future inflation and pay awards is to be included in the budget. There is also the question of whether provision needs to be made for things like sickness cover, maternity leave, etc. When estimating costs you should work from the basis that:

Cost = Price x Quantity

So in the case of the hire of training rooms, for example, the price per room per day needs to be multiplied by the number of rooms estimated to be needed during the year. Before you can determine price or quantity you need to have considered the quality of resource input required, such as the quality of the training rooms, and the quality/experience required of the trainer. Remember to consider whether the current price for a training room needs to be raised for inflation.

When estimating salaries it is important to remember that the cost of employing someone is not just the cost of their salary. There are also the employer on-costs of national insurance and, where appropriate, superannuation. With a small unit you are likely to work from the basis of people's actual grade and their 'point' on the scale of that grade. In large departments salaries may be estimated on the basis of the grade for the job and the number of people on that grade. Rather than take people's actual point on the scale in the latter case the 'law of averages' will be employed and the mid-point for the grade used instead.

Estimating the budget becomes a little more complicated where pay awards occur part-way through the year and when the unit plans to expand or contract part-way through the year. In these instances you need to calculate the part-year effects of changes occurring during the year. When you plan budgets for reasonably large units you need to consider the implication of staff turnover. It is normal not to have all posts filled all of the time. It is quite usual for the organization as a whole to apply a vacancy rate assumption when trying to estimate their resource costs for the forthcoming year. Thus the budget for salaries might be reduced by 4 per cent, say, across the board as an estimate of the reduction in resource costs due to vacancies. CIPFA (1991, p.33) provide the following checklist for constructing staff budgets.

You should make sure that you include the following items in your budgets for salaried staff:

— increments
— regradings
— pay awards
— allowances
— vacancy factors (or staff turnover) and their effect on increments and pay awards
— overtime (if applicable)
— local pay weightings
— provision for annual leave or sickness cover
— different pay rates for weekend working or anti-social hours
— agency staff

In some cases it may not be easy to use the formula of Cost = Price x Quantity, because you do not have the required information for one or both of the elements. For example, it may be difficult for you to estimate central service charges in this way. Traditionally the costs of central services have been allocated to service department budgets on the basis of apportionment. That is, the total cost of operating the central services is estimated. These costs are then apportioned to each user budget on a pro-rata basis. So in the case of payroll costs this may be allocated to each user budget on the basis of the number of employees. Our training unit has four members of staff, the whole local authority has 12,000 staff so their share of the payroll costs would be 4/12,000 (only 0.03 per cent). Such apportionment of central service costs is becoming less frequent, particularly in local government. In its place central service departments are setting up service level agreements with the users of their services. These service agreements specify the quantity and type of service to be provided for a given cost.

So far we have just been talking about the training unit budget as if it were only concerned with costs. There is also the question of estimating income. The most likely form of income would be the fees charged to those who attended the training unit's courses. At one time such courses may have been provided as if they were free of charge. Of course there was still a cost associated with them, but this was not directly charged to those who attended the courses. In these instances the training unit would have been seen as another central service and its costs would have been apportioned to users on a pro-rata basis (possibly on the basis of the number of employees). In the current climate of the internal trading of support services it is unlikely that the training unit would be centrally funded in this way; more likely it would have to earn all or part of its expenditure requirements by directly charging users for its courses (and any other services it might provide).

Having taken all the above factors into account Figure 10.5 shows the budget estimate for the fictional training unit.

Figure 10.6: *Training unit budget for 199X/199Y*

	£
Expenditure	
Employees	
Salaries	78,433
(incl. NI & Superannuation)	
Travel	1,250
Supplies & Services	
Hire of training venues	15,000
Outside trainer fees	10,000
Stationery, photocopying, postage	7,500
Central service cost	6,500
(incl. office accommodation costs)	
Total expenditure	118,683
Income	120,000

Because of the time-consuming nature of constructing a budget from 'scratch' for all parts of a large organization every year, it is common to adopt the short cut known as *incremental budgeting*. This is the process by which the budget for the following year is built up incrementally from the budget for the current year (the base budget). So:

Base budget + Inflation + Committed growth + New growth - savings = Next year's budget

Because of the nature of the process, it is sometimes referred to as rolling forward last year's budget. The advantages of incremental budgeting include:

- It is a relatively straightforward process — only the marginal changes need to be understood and agreed
- It is relatively inexpensive as a budgetary process as less time is spent on preparing the budget
- Many activities are mandatory or fundamental and continue year in year out, hence it is sensible to concentrate on the marginal changes from what has gone before
- It leads to change in small steps and hence avoids making serious mistakes
- It has proved to be politically and organizationally acceptable

The disadvantages of incremental budgeting include:

- The greater part of the budget moves forward unquestioned because there is relatively little attention to justifying the base budget
- The emphasis is on monetary inputs rather than the objectives which those inputs are meant to achieve
- The budget relates to past rather than future priorities
- It leads to a tendency to spend up to the limit of this year's budget in order to maximize next year's budget

Although the drawbacks of incremental budgeting are readily recognized it has proved difficult to find workable alternatives to it. Starting from scratch each year, which is the basis on which the training unit budget (referred to above) has been built is known as zero-based budgeting, because it starts from a zero base[1]. Zero-based budgeting has proved to be unworkable as a system of budgeting for the whole organization every year.

A complementary approach to budgetary planning and allocation, which is increasing in use, is the process of using resource allocation formulae. Once a budget for a service area has been established, usually on an incremental basis, this budget is distributed to the component parts of the service by using an allocation formula.

---

[1] Fully fledged zero-based budgeting not only assumes that you start from zero in constructing the budget, it also requires that you consider the costs of alternative forms and level of service delivery and structure these in the form of decision packages. For a full explanation of zero-based budgeting *see* Jones and Pendlebury (1992), Chapter 5.

In the case of the total schools' budget, for example, a formula based on pupil numbers (weighted for age and other factors) would be used to distribute the total budget among the schools in the area.

How are resources allocated and budgets decided in your own organization? Talk to your line manager and the accountant responsible for your area about each of the following approaches to budgeting and the extent to which they are utilized in your organization:

— *incremental budgeting*
— *resource allocation formulae*
— *zero-based budgeting*
— *other budgetary systems?*

As a result of your discussions produce a written description of the budgetary planning process adopted by your organization.

Costing units of service

There are two main reasons why it is becoming more important to be able to cost individual units of service (e.g. the cost of educating one pupil or the cost of a hip replacement operation):

1. accountability, that is, being able to provide cost information as part of the demonstration of an efficient provision of service (see Chapter 8)
2. tendering and charging for service provision

The usual method for costing individual units of service in the public sector is known as unit costing. This is a fairly crude approach where the total cost of providing a service is divided by the number of units provided. So if, say, the total cost of a liver transplant unit was £1,950,000 for the year and the number of operations conducted was 100, then the unit cost would be £1,950,000/100 = £19,500 per operation.

What are the problems with this as a means of costing individual liver transplantation operations?

One of the main problems with such unit costing is that it is an average cost which is likely to mask a wide variety of actual costs. The level of service provided for each liver transplant patient may be highly variable with some patients remaining in hospital for a short period whilst others are there for much longer periods. In addition such an average unit cost would not be of any help in deciding whether to treat one more patient; that is, it does not reflect the cost of treating one more patient (which is known as the marginal cost).

The aim of a costing system is to charge as accurately as possible to each *chosen unit* the cost incurred in producing it. Costing systems are used to aid planning, control and decision-making. Each of these purposes requires a different approach to costing and these differing approaches are considered below. In the above definition we referred to the *chosen unit*; the boundary of the unit of product or service which you wish to cost can be drawn at a number of levels:

Functions	e.g.	Education
		Highways
Cost centres	e.g.	Schools
		Direct labour organizations
Cost units	e.g.	Pupils
		Jobs

However the boundary of the unit of service you wish to cost is drawn, it is important to consider two approaches to costing:

— Absorption costing
— Marginal costing

Both of these are discussed below.

Absorption costing

Absorption costing is the traditional approach to costing in the public sector. It requires that all costs are absorbed at the level of the unit of service which is being costed (e.g. the liver transplant operation). When we say *all* costs we are referring to both direct and indirect costs:

1. Direct costs are directly traceable to the unit of service being costed
2. Indirect costs are sometimes referred to as overheads; They cannot be directly attributed to a service, and so have to be apportioned on some equitable basis

The classification of something as a direct or indirect cost is always from the point of view of the object being costed. For example, if the unit of service being costed is a leisure centre, then the direct costs are likely to include all the staff who work at the leisure centre, the supplies which they use, along with their heating, lighting and other building-related costs. The indirect costs are likely to include the central management and administration services provided by the Leisure Services Department. If, however, it is the cost of the swimming pool within this leisure centre which is our cost object, then the direct costs are likely to include only any supplies which are purchased solely for use within the swimming pool, together with any staff who are employed solely to work in relation to the swimming pool. All the other previously categorized direct costs become indirect costs as they are now costs which need to be shared equitably amongst all the facilities within the leisure centre (e.g. part of the heating bill needs to be apportioned to the swimming pool).

In the case of the liver transplantation unit

- The direct costs are likely to include:

    — medical and nursing salaries
    — the salaries of other staff directly working for the unit

- equipment servicing
- medical and surgical supplies
- diagnostic tests and services
- cost of transporting organs

- The indirect costs are likely to include:
    - premises-related costs (e.g. heating and lighting)
    - central management and administrative costs
    - 'hotel' services (e.g. catering, laundry and cleaning)
    - portering

A distinction might be made between indirect costs and other overhead costs. For example the NHS Management Executive (1990) provide the following indicative cost classification:

- Direct costs
    - Facility costs — e.g. ward, medical and nursing staff involved
    - Diagnostic costs in support departments (radiology, pathology)
    - Drug costs
    - Operating theatre costs
    - Other miscellaneous paramedical direct treatment expenditure
    - Miscellaneous patient treatment services
    - Research and Development Programmes

- Indirect costs (in support of direct patient care)
    - Catering expenditure
    - Laundry expenditure
    - Linen expenditure
    - Medical record expenditure
    - Miscellaneous services and supplies
    - Teaching programmes

- Other overhead expenditure
    - Administration and management
    - Training and education
    - Domestic and cleaning
    - Portering
    - Transport expenditure
    - Estate management expenditure
    - Other services

- Capital costs
    - Interest charges
    - Depreciation charges (which can be defined as the loss in value of an asset, such as a major item of equipment) over a period of time

The indirect costs, overhead costs and capital charges from this classification list can all be subsumed under our overall heading of indirect costs.

Continuing with the liver transplantation example, as direct costs are, by definition, directly traceable to liver transplantation they can be attributed to that unit. The indirect costs are shared with the other treatment units within the hospital and hence a basis for apportioning or allocating these costs to the liver transplantation unit is needed. A number of different bases of apportionment might be used:

1. The number of beds — for, say, laundry and linen costs
2. The number of staff — for certain central administration costs, like administration of the payroll
3. The floor space of the unit — for, say, cleaning costs

Marginal costing

A marginal costing approach is concerned with identifying how costs behave (change) with changes in the level of activity. More specifically it is concerned with the marginal (additional) cost of providing one more unit of service. In order to be able to assess marginal cost, the main distinction to be drawn in terms of cost behaviour is between fixed and variable costs:

1. Fixed costs do not change with the level of activity
2. Variable costs vary according to activity, thus if activity increases by 20%, the variable cost increases by 20%.

In the case of the liver transplantation unit example:

1. the fixed costs are likely to include certain of the direct cost, such as medical and nursing salaries, and the indirect costs
2. the variable costs are likely to include drugs, other medical and surgical supplies, and diagnostic tests.

The difference between fixed and variable costs may be clear in theory, but it is often difficult to apply in practice. Many so-called fixed costs may really be semi-fixed. An example of a semi-fixed cost might be teachers' salaries. A school could have an increase in activity, (number of pupils) without needing to spend more on teachers' salaries; hence they appear to be a fixed cost. However, if the number of pupils increases beyond an acceptable pupil-to-teacher ratio, then additional teaching staff will need to be employed. Similarly, in the liver transplant example, medical and nursing salaries will be a semi-fixed cost. They may not increase if 105 as opposed to 100 operations are done in a year, but if the activity of the unit is increased by 50 per cent to 150 operations per year, present staffing levels are unlikely to be sufficient.

Despite the difficulty of classifying costs as either fixed or variable, the distinction is a useful one. Where decisions need to be made about whether to increase or decrease the level of service offered, an important factor will be the cost implications of doing either of these things. It is highly unlikely that if the service level is increased by 20 per cent, the cost of the service will also increase by 20 per cent. To work out the additional cost, an analysis which classifies costs according to whether they are fixed or variable is required. A simple example will illustrate this.

A catering service has been asked to consider the cost of increasing the number of meals it produces per week from 500 to 600.

The variable costs per meal are:

Food	50p
Fuel, etc.	20p
The fixed costs per annum are:	
Wages	£16,000
Overheads	£12,000

So the current cost per annum of producing 500 meals per week (every week of the year) are:

Variable cost per meal	70p	
Number of meals per year	26,000	
Variable cost per annum		
(70p x 26,000)		£18,200
Fixed costs per annum		£28,000
Total cost		£46,200

The present catering staff can cope with the increase from 500 to 600 meals and the other overheads will not vary with the increase. So the cost of producing 600 meals per week (without taking account of any future inflation) is:

Variable cost per meal	70p	
Number of meals per year	31,200	
Variable cost per annum		
(70p x 31,200)		£21,840
Fixed costs per annum		£28,000
Total cost		£49,840

So the 20 per cent increase in activity only leads to an increase in cost of approximately 8 per cent.

In instances where the service is *not* already working to capacity, the marginal cost of providing a service to one more customer is equivalent to the variable cost per customer.

The application of a marginal costing approach can go further than outlined above by taking revenue into account. The key questions which can then be answered are: how much does the revenue from a service contribute towards the recovery of fixed costs?, at what volume of activity and/or at what price per service unit will the service break even (that is, revenue will equal costs)? A detailed discussion of the methods employed in answering these questions is beyond the scope of this chapter. Those wishing to read further should consult Chapter 3 of Coombs and Jenkins (1991).

Defining appropriate units of service for costing purposes

One of the problems of costing units of public sector service is their lack of homogeneity (i.e. different levels of service are provided according to differing needs) and hence it is important to define appropriate units of service for costing purposes in order to reflect this diversity. Some examples of possible units of service are:

1. Cost per hour of service (e.g. financial services, home care services)
2. Cost per consultation (e.g. education psychology)
3. Cost per treatment (e.g. removal of ingrowing toe nail by chiropodist, removal of wasps' nest by environmental health officer)
4. Cost per bed per day (e.g. place in a residential home).

As public sector services move away from contracting for the provision of service on the basis of a block contract (see Chapter 8) towards a cost per case basis, there will be an even greater need to consider the appropriate definition of the unit of service to be costed and charged for. For example, a home help service would need to be wary of contracting on the basis of the number of homes to be served, when the amount of service to be provided at each home might vary from one hour to six hours per day.

Now consider your own area of public sector service. What are the items of direct cost associated with your service area? Do you know the level of these for the present financial year?

What are the indirect costs associated with your service area? Do you know the level of these costs for the present financial year? How have they been apportioned to you?

If asked to estimate the cost of your service, as a basis for charging for this service, what would be an appropriate unit of service to cost?

You may have had some problems with the questions relating to your knowledge of particular costs for the current financial year. The form of existing financial information is frequently ill-suited to answering such questions, as many of the existing financial information systems were designed for accountancy, rather than service management, purposes. Take this opportunity to discuss these problems with your line manager and the accountant responsible for advising your service area.

Conclusions

This chapter has argued that increasingly public sector managers need to develop financial management skills. It has reviewed the main financial management skills and concepts relating to budgetary planning and management, and followed this by a consideration of the main approaches to costing units of service. The main conclusions to be drawn from this chapter are:

- Good financial management skills rest on the ability to interpret a wide range of financial information statements

- In order to be able to interpret such statements the standard structures of these statements and the processes which lie behind them need to be understood.

It is possible to develop these skills and the requisite level of understanding without having to train as an accountant. The first barrier to overcome is the language used to describe financial management ideas. Many of these ideas follow the line of common sense and so can be understood. The technical language, or jargon, is a shorthand way of referring to a commonsense process. Crack the jargon and you are halfway there. After working your way through this chapter you should already have picked up some of the language and ideas necessary to beginning this process.

References

CIPFA (1991) *Community Care '91: Managing the Money*, Chartered Institute of Public Finance and Accountancy.

JONES, R. and PENDLEBURY, M. (1992) *Public Sector Accounting*, Pitman.

NHS MANAGEMENT EXECUTIVE (1990), quoted in S. ELLWOOD (1992) *Cost Methods for NHS Healthcare Contracts*, Chartered Institute of Management Accountants.

PERRIN, J. (1988), *Resource Management in the NHS*, Van Nonstrand Reinhold.

Guided reading

An excellent book which explores in detail all the topics covered in this chapter and more is:

COOMBS, H.M. and JENKINS, D.E. (1991) *Public Sector Financial Management*, Chapman & Hall.

It is worth contacting the professional body (or bodies) involved in your service area for any financial management training material they may provide. It is also worth contacting the Chartered Institute of Public Finance and Accountancy (CIPFA) for their training packs. For example, CIPFA provide a very useful financial training pack in relation to the impact of the community care legislation:

CIPFA (1991), *Community Care '91: Managing the Money*, Chartered Institute of Public Finance and Accountancy.

If you want to know more about the financial and accounting arrangements in various parts of the public sector, then a good starting point is:

HENLEY, D., LIKIERMAN, A., PERRIN, J., EVANS, M., LAPSLEY, I. and WHITEOAK, J. (1992) *Public Sector Accounting and Financial Control*, Chapman & Hall.

Chapter 11:
Making information work for you

Ever-increasing amounts of information are given to and required by managers at all levels within the public sector. If managers are not to become overwhelmed by this information they need to be able to make sense of it and its implications, organize and prioritize which information is going to be acted upon and when. They also need to ensure that they are getting the information they need to meet their responsibilities. The purpose of this chapter is to enable you to begin this process. By the end of the chapter you should:

- be able to describe what management information means and why it is important
- be clearer about your own information needs and the extent to which these are met at present
- understand the stages in designing and managing information systems
- be clearer about the ways in which information technology can assist in the management of information

Whilst reading this chapter it is worth remembering the point made in Chapter 3 (on power), that information and information control provide an important base of power. This may help to explain why information is not always shared as freely as a rational analysis might suggest it should be.

What is information?

When you hear the term 'management information' what do you think of? What is management information?

It is common for textbooks to distinguish between data and information. Data are unanalyzed facts and figures. Management information is data that have been analyzed and made meaningful for managers. A list of financial transactions during the last month is data; a budgetary control statement, which analyzes these transactions, matches them against budget headings and calculates the difference between planned spend and actual spend, is management information. Such information is used to support four key management tasks: planning, co-ordinating, decision-making and control. An information system is a set of procedures designed routinely to collect, process, store and disseminate information.

What information systems are available within your organization? How does your organization make use of them? How useful do you find them?

It should be possible to identify a number of information systems. For example, there should be a financial information system which provides you with budgetary and cost information. There is likely to be a personnel information system which provides you with information about employees, pay scales, holidays, overtime, and so on. There may be a number of information systems relating to your service users, such a records of visits, progress on rehabilitation programmes, and records of service charge payments.

The comments of many managers within the public sector suggest that many of the information systems which support their activities are not always as useful as they would like. This may be because systems primarily designed for one purpose (e.g. financial accounting) have been only partly adapted to meet other purposes (financial management information). Where systems are criticized it is likely that they fail to meet the requirements of useful information; that is, the information they provide should be:

- timely — the information being available in time for it to be acted upon
- appropriate — to the manager's needs
- accurate and adequately detailed
- understandable

Ideally an information system should start from the basis of storing information that meets operational needs. If those working at the operational level find such a system useful, they are more likely to ensure that the data which is entered is accurate and timely. Such a starting point is appropriate, because management information is usually a summary of operational information.

A good information system should flag up points where action is required, it should also identify problems by highlighting where the data collected indicates that activities have fallen outside acceptable parameters. It will then have routines which ensure that information about potential problems is communicated to the appropriate person. A good system should also only gather the information it needs, rather than recording everything which is available.

What information is communicated to whom is likely to vary according to their level in the management hierarchy, with front-line managers requiring detailed, current and mainly operational information, whilst more senior managers require summarized, medium-term and strategic information. Figure 11.1 illustrates this by looking at the monitoring information needed by managers at different levels within the organization. The information which is communicated will also vary according to whether it is directly accessible to the individual, or whether it is provided to him/her (and hence filtered) by another person.

Figure 11.1: *Responsibilities for monitoring*

Different managers need different information

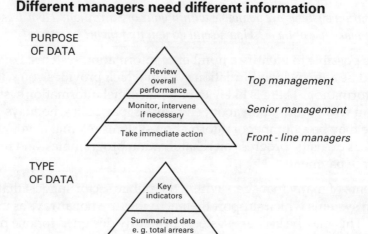

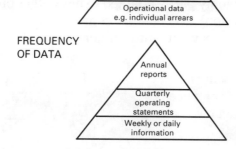

Source: Audit Commission (1988) *Performance Review in Local Government: Action Guide*, Audit Commission, p.6.

Another useful distinction to make when considering information is the difference between 'hard' and 'soft' information. Hard information might be the facts and figures available to you about your service users. Soft information may be the knowledge that a certain day centre is the pet project of the chair of the committee which oversees the work of your unit. Information systems, nowadays, tend to be seen in terms of computerized systems. Whilst such information technology has been important in the development of information systems, there is still a role for 'soft'/manual systems.

What are your information needs?

Let us begin to answer the above question by first of all considering your present use of information and the extent to which the information you receive is adequate and appropriate.

Try to keep a diary for a week of all the pieces of information which come to you. This might include: financial information relating to budgets, information about service users, details relating to government policies, information about proposed internal restructuring, press clippings relating to your area of work, details of new publications relating to your area of work, information about training opportunities. It may also include the information you obtain by regularly accessing computerized information systems. At the end of the week, first of all produce a tally of the extent to which the information you received can be categorized as hard or soft. Then try to produce a profile of the information you receive by using the categories below:

Time-scale of usefulness	Primarily useful for				Of little or no foreseeable use
	Planning	Co-ordinating	Decision-making	Control	
Short term					
Medium term					
Long term					

For each piece of information put a tick in the box most appropriate to the use you might make of this information. If necessary, ticks can be placed in more than one box where a piece of information serves a number of uses. So, if a memo is received giving you the latest population projection for your area, you might decide that this is useful for long-term planning and hence a tick is placed in the bottom left-hand box. When you have completed the categorization, produce a tally of the number of ticks in each box. Are the ticks evenly distributed? What sorts of information appear to be the most prevalent? Are there any types of information which are underrepresented, and would you expect to receive information in these areas? Is the reason for their absence due to this being an untypical week? Finally what proportion of the information you received have you deemed to be of little or no foreseeable use?

The above exercise should help you to begin the process of auditing your receipt and use of information. The answers to the questions may suggest areas where you need more information. The exercise may also serve to highlight areas where the information need not be addressed to you (and may in fact be redirected to a more appropriate person). This latter point leads us on to consider how information is used in your unit as a whole.

Choose five pieces of the information noted in your diary. For each piece of information try to develop a profile of how it is used within the unit you work in. Do this by producing five charts similar to that shown in Figure 11.2. This will involve you in analysing the extent to which individuals within your unit use the information available. Does this profile suggest that your unit is handling information in the most efficient and effective way? Is it clear to the individuals involved what they should be doing with this information? Is there another way of sharing information and directing it to those who need it?

Reflect on the results of the above exercises and begin to think more broadly about the information needs of your unit. Is there a gap between the information you require in the process of planning, making decision, co-ordinating and controlling activities in the achievement of your objectives, and the information which is available? Try to list what you see as the gaps. Such gaps may relate to the information you need to receive about the services provided by other units/departments to your service users.

Figure 11.2: *Profile of information use*

WHAT RECIPIENT DOES WITH THE INFORMATION	Person A	Person B	Person C	Person D	Person E
Uses for decision-making					
Uses for evaluation				✓	
Uses for planning					
Uses for influencing					
Uses for own information					
Collates or summarizes	✓				
Looks at					
Passes on		✓			✓
Places in bin					
Receives	✓	✓	✓	✓	✓

PASSAGE OF PIECE OF INFORMATION

Source: Adapted from D. Torrington, J. Weightman and K. Johns (1989), *Effective Management*, Prentice Hall p. 342.

You may be tempted to call for all information gaps to be filled. You need to remember, however, that information costs money. There is the time taken to collect data, analyze it and then present it in a form useful to managers. There may be a cost associated with the collection of data — for example, survey costs. Another cost can be the technology which is needed to store, retrieve and analyse the data collected (this is the subject of the section on 'Using information technology'. below). A further cost will be the time that managers spend receiving and considering the increased amounts of information provided for them.

If existing information does not match your requirements it may be possible to think of ways in which existing information can be used to provide new information, that is, by collating it and analyzing it in different ways. For example, a hospital management team may require patient load information relating to particular speciality areas. Rather than establishing a new system within each of the speciality areas to capture this information, it may be possible to 'rebundle' information from a general patient information system. Similarly, a residential services officer may require information on the dependency levels of the service users. This need not necessarily entail a survey of all service users, it may be possible to use existing information systems to assess and/or estimate dependency levels.

This naturally leads us on to consider the information systems which are available to you. Frequently the information you might need in your role as a manager may be available within the organization, but it may not be easily accessible. For example, the information may be found by 'leafing' through a hundred case file notes, but it is not available at 'the touch of a button'. Alternatively the information you require may be there in the form of twenty pages of computer printout, but not in a way which you find easy to use or digest.

It is worth spending some time considering the information you most require for the day-to-day running of your service and then looking at ways in which this information might be made more accessible. It is also worth while considering how the information can be made more digestible. This may entail giving one person the task of analyzing and summarizing the implications of a particular piece of information. It may also entail designing systems in such a way as to ensure that potential problems are easily identifiable. Examples of this are variance analysis and exception reporting. We have already discussed variance analysis in Chapter 10 when we looked at budgetary control. Variance analysis compares planned with actual results and notes the extent of their difference. Exception reporting tries to overcome the problem of having to wade through a mass of information, which is basically telling you that all is fine, in order to discover a problem that is buried within this information. An exception reporting system would only provide information on those items which had gone outside the predetermined boundaries of acceptability.

Information systems may be manual (e.g. card files), but more frequently they will draw upon the power of the computer to enable information to be stored, retrieved, updated and analyzed quickly. This is the subject of the next section, but before moving on to this, it is worth outlining the key concepts and stages in designing a management information system.

There are three main stages to consider:
- The first stage in the design of a management information system is to be clear about why a system is needed; what objectives it is meant to achieve. As we have discussed in previous chapters, systems can be described in terms of three main components:

    Inputs ⟶ Process ⟶ Outputs

The first stage is, thus, defining the required outputs and why they are needed.

- The second stage will consider the input side of the system: what 'raw' data is needed and how it can be collected/accessed.
- The third stage considers the processing of this information: how it should be classified (coded) and what combinations or analyses of raw data are needed to provide the outputs required.

The above three stages enable a detailed specification of the information system requirements to be produced. At this point it should be possible to judge whether the information system should be manual or whether the processing power of a computer is required.

Many information systems are more complex than the simple systems model outlined above implies. They may in fact be an amalgam of several such systems, where the output from one system becomes the input for another. As a result, the information flows around the system may be quite complex and require careful mapping. The example on page 173 will help to illustrate this.

Figure 11.3: *Criminal Justice System agency interactions*

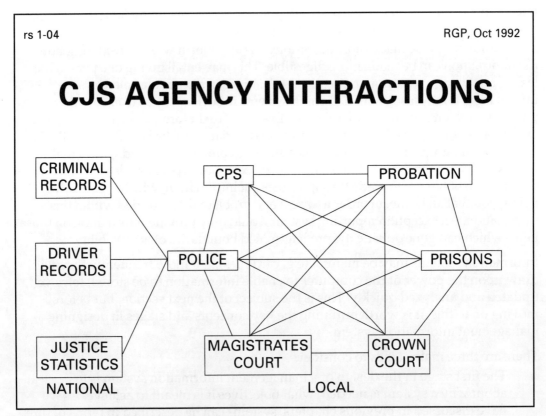

Key: CJS = Criminal Justice System
CPS = Crown Prosecution Service
Source: Northumbrian Probation Service.

A probation service has an information system which monitors and co-ordinates information on each case referred to it by the courts. Keeping such a system up-to-date requires complex flows of information amongst a number of criminal justice agencies, as Figure 11.3 illustrates. For example, the police provide information on arrests and cautioning, the courts provide information on appearances in court and the results of these appearances. These and other details are co-ordinated on the case/client data base, which also feeds information back to both the police and the courts. The police are given parole details, and the courts receive reports and standard letters with regard to clients appearing before them.

Using information technology

Information technology (often shortened to IT) is the technology concerned with the processing of information. It covers computer hardware (machines) and software (programmes that tell machines what to do), telecommunications and other office equipment.

The speed of the development of IT has been phenomenal. The technology for IT becomes 30 per cent cheaper each year and its power (in terms of its capacity to handle information and the speed at which it does this) has increased a thousandfold since the 1970s. It is set to improve by another thousandfold over the next ten to fifteen years.[1] Such a rapid development in the capacity to handle information and the reduction of the cost of purchasing ever more sophisticated hardware and software, means that IT has had a major impact on organizational life.

In what ways does your organization currently use information technology? List some common uses. What impact has it had on organizational life?

The positive impacts and potential of IT can be grouped under:

- Greater access to and sharing of information — for example, up-to-date information on service users can be shared simultaneously by a number of employees, units and departments.
- Greater possibility for decentralizing decision-making — if more information is available locally it may be possible to delegate more decision-making to the local level. No longer do decisions need to be made by the centres, which are no longer the only places in the organizations where information is brought together.
- Greater possibility for combining and analyzing data from different information sources — combining and analyzing manual information is very time-consuming. Providing that the IT system has sufficient flexibility in its design, such combination and analysis become a realistic possibility.

[1] These statistics were quoted by Dr G. Robinson in a lecture delivered to the RSA on 4 December 1991, 'NSA: The Networked Society for the Arts, Manufactures and Commerce', reproduced in *RSA Journal*, **5428**, April 1992, pp. 305–20.

These impacts affect not only the employees of an organization, but also its service users. IT can be seen positively in terms of enhancing access, choices and participation, but there is a down-side to this, the concerns relating to the privacy of information and its ethical use. The Data Protection Act 1984 aims to limit the potential for misuse of personal information held on computers. Any computer system holding confidential personal data must be registered, and it is a requirement of the Act that any person recorded in the system has a right to see the information being held about him/her. The eight main principles of the Data Protection Act are:

1. Obtain and process data fairly and lawfully
2. Hold data only for the purposes specified in your Register entry
3. Only use the data for the purposes registered, and disclose it only to the people listed in your Register entry
4. Hold only data which is adequate, relevant and not excessive in relation to the purpose for which it is held
5. Ensure personal data is adequate for the registered purpose and, where necessary, kept up-to-date
6. Hold it for no longer than is necessary
7. Allow individuals access to information held about them and, where appropriate correct or erase it
8. Take security measures to prevent unauthorized or accidental access to, or alteration, disclosure, or loss and destruction of personal information

In addition to linking into organization-wide information systems by the use of local computer terminals or a personal computer link, many managers now have the advantage of using their own personal computer. The main software packages (which can be purchased 'off the shelf') which managers will find useful are:

- Word-processing packages — such as *Word Perfect* or *Word*, which provide a flexible means of producing memos, letters, reports, etc., in standard or individual format.
- Spreadsheet packages — such as *Lotus 123* or *Supercalc*, which provide a table-like format of rows and columns into which text or figures can be entered. The figures can be added, subtracted, multiplied, etc. The data can remain in tabular form or can be converted into a graphical presentation, such as a bar chart. For example, data might be entered into the spreadsheet on the hours teachers spend in class room contact for various subject areas. The spreadsheet can then be used to calculate total teaching hours for both the individual teachers and the subject areas. Additional data might be added on the number of pupils in each subject area, and a teacher–pupil ratio calculated.
- Database packages — such as *Dbase* or *Dataease*, which provide a means of storing records on a case-by-case basis. This data base of information can be interrogated to answer questions such as, which service users are one-parent families living in housing association accommodation.

With the continuing rapid development of the capacity and capabilities of IT it is likely that you will continue to be involved with questions relating to the introduction of new IT systems. The next section aims to provide you with some guidelines for such situations.

Stages in introducing IT

Planning for the introduction of IT is often seen as a linear and rational process. A good example of this is Fairbairn's (1982) ten-point plan for the selection of a system:

1. Needs are defined
2. Alternatives to computer applications are examined
3. Quantities in relation to file size, time-scales and access requirements are defined
4. Software is explored
5. Hardware alternatives are considered
6. Software and hardware are evaluated
7. Expansion capability is considered
8. Suppliers are compared
9. Support and maintenance is considered
10. Installation is scheduled

Whilst these stages are important, you also need to consider the politics of the change process and the resistance to change which can occur (*see* Chapter 12).

Think of any experience you have had of the introduction of IT. Did the process run smoothly? If not why not?

Some common pitfalls are:

- separation of users of IT systems from those who design them which means that users' needs are not adequately met
- lack of consideration of human reactions to IT developments (fears of deskilling and redundancy, as well as fears of having to use the technology itself)
- lack of user training leading to the misuse or under-use of IT systems
- the purchase of inadequate 'off the shelf' systems which cannot be adapted to local needs
- inadequate supplier support which causes problems where the computer system 'goes down'
- decision to design and produce in-house software without a proper appreciation of the time and expense involved
- lack of consideration of the effect on the existing balance of power within the organization (e.g. more people may now have access to information which was formerly the domain of one person)

As IT becomes ever more sophisticated it is likely to be more beneficial for an individual organization to buy 'off the shelf' software rather than try to develop its own. Some public sector organizations have formed consortia to share the costs and the benefits of developing their own software. The qualities an organization should consider when making an 'off the shelf' purchase include the extent to which the software is flexible enough to be adapted for local needs and the level of after-purchase supplier support.

There is a danger that the installation of IT may be pursued for its own sake and systems introduced because computerization is seen as a 'good thing'. The objectives and benefits of computerization always need to be clearly specified and it should not be assumed that computerization is innately beneficial. The experience of introducing IT in the public sector suggests that the costs of IT are often underestimated and the benefits not fully explored or achieved:

> Research studies suggest that about 20 per cent of UK IT expenditure is wasted, and that between 30–40 per cent of IT projects realise no net benefits whatsoever, however measured.
>
> (Willcocks, 1992, p.171)

Conclusions

This chapter should have helped you explore your own management information needs and the extent to which these needs are being met at present. It should also have helped you consider the extent to which your existing information systems are adequate or whether they need to be developed.

The conclusion is that information and the appropriate management of it are vital to all managers. You need to ensure that you are getting the right information and are not being overwhelmed by information which is only indirectly relevant to your tasks. Information is only useful if it is used, and used for the right purposes. IT can help you manage information in an efficient and effective manner, but it is not a magic solution to all information problems. There are many pitfalls to avoid in introducing IT and you need to remember that any system is only as good as the data fed into it. As the saying goes, 'rubbish in, rubbish out'.

References

AUDIT COMMISSION (1988), *Performance Review in Local Government: Action Guide*, Audit Commission.

FAIRBAIRN, D. (1982) Chapter 10 in RANK XEROX, *Brave New World?*, Macdonald.

ROBINSON, Dr G. (1992) 'NSA: The Networked Society for the Arts, Manufacturers and Commerce' *RSA Journal*, April.

TORRINGTON, D., WEIGHTMAN, J. and JOHNS, K. (1989) *Effective Management: People and Organisation*, Prentice-Hall.

WILLCOCKS, L. (1992) 'The manager as technologist', Chapter 7 in L. WILLCOCKS and J. HARROW (eds.), *Rediscovering Public Services Management*, McGraw-Hill.

Guided reading

A more detailed discussion of management information systems can be found in:

LUCEY, T. (1987) *Management Information Systems*, D P Publications.

MARTIN, C. and POWELL, P. (1994) *Information Systems: a Management Perspective*, McGraw-Hill.

The use and potential abuse of IT is explored in Chapters 7 and 10 of:

WILLCOCKS, L. and HARROW, J. (eds.) (1992) *Rediscovering Public Services Management*, McGraw-Hill.

Also see:

ISAAC-HENRY, K. (1993), 'The management of information technology in the public sector', in K. ISAAC-HENRY, C. PAINTER and C. BARNES (eds.), *Management in the Public Sector: Challenge and Change*, Chapman & Hall.

Chapter 12:
Managing during times of change

In the very first chapter of this book we asked you to think about those changes which have occurred in your organization in the recent past as well as those which appear to be on the horizon in the future. At that point we were interested in trying to categorize the changes in order to see if it was possible to group and characterize them. Now we want to focus more squarely on the process by which change occurs and its consequences for managing within organizations during times of relatively major change. In particular we are concerned with the effect of change on people and how the worst of these effects might be alleviated. Chapter 6 (Developing new services) has already considered the process of innovation and how this process might be managed. The present chapter should serve to enhance and complement the ideas introduced there.

By the end of this chapter you should:

- be better able to describe the different degrees of change
- be clearer about the process by which change occurs
- understand why lasting change might be difficult to achieve in public sector organizations
- have considered the stages, activities and skills involved in planning and managing change
- be aware of the effects of change on people and how the worst of these might be eliminated.

Understanding the change process

Before moving on to consider managing during times of change, let us first consider what we mean by this thing called organizational change. Change in itself is a difficult concept to get hold of.

How would you describe 'organizational change'? How would you know when it had occurred?

If change is seen as the opposite of stability and if we envisage organizations as open systems (as discussed in Chapter 1), which are constantly interacting with a dynamic environment, then change will be seen as a constant feature of organizations. What will need explaining in these circumstances is not change, but why there is apparent stability. It, therefore, makes sense to talk of change in relative terms, that is, of the different degrees of change. The need to use some form of adjective to define the degree of change is reinforced when we think how broadly the term 'change' is used. Handy (1981) points out that change is used to describe the trivial 'a change of clothes' as well as the profound 'a change of life'. So how do we begin to categorize the differing degrees of change? Wilson (1992) provides one such categorization; he refers to four different degrees of change:

- *status quo* — no change in current practice
- *expanded reproduction* — change involves producing more of the same (goods or services)
- *evolutionary transition* — change occurs within existing parameters of the organization. That is, although there is change, by and large the existing structure and systems are retained.
- *revolutionary transformation* — change involves shifting or redefining existing parameters. This means that structure and systems are likely to change.

We might surmise that the process by which change occurs (that is, the *how* rather than the *what* of change) is affected by the degree of change occurring. With expanded reproduction the main change is the increased size of the organization, as it grows to produce more of the same services. Many public sector organizations during the 1960s and early 1970s experienced change of this nature — more schools, hospitals, council houses and libraries were built to cope with the increasing demand for public sector services. These new facilities tended to fit within existing, if expanded regimes. The change which occurred tended to relate to fragmentation (or differentiation) as jobs and departments split into sub-units, each with its own specific tasks in order to cope with the increasing volume of work. Not all the changes occurring at this time were about producing more of the same. There were also new services being introduced (such as community development) and others were being amended (such as the conversion of grammar and secondary schools into comprehensive schools). However, during times of growth, the easiest way to accommodate change is to add onto the existing structure. So, generally, community development grew up alongside the existing community services provided by Education, Social Work and Leisure Services Departments. These additions led, over time, to a change in the overall orientation of the organization and it is possible to characterize this process as one of evolution. Within this evolutionary process amendments to existing ways of operating tended to be introduced via incremental adjustments.

This is not to say that more radical or fundamental changes did not occur in the public sector during the 1960s and early 1970s. However, attempts to introduce more of a revolutionary transformation rarely seemed to have the impact which was intended. Take, for example, the somewhat abortive attempts to introduce corporate management into local government after the 1974 reorganization of local authorities. Although corporate structures, management teams and council committees were introduced, the comment of many was that departmental concerns were still the primary focus of chief officers and committee members and many of the corporate structures (such as cross-departmental planning and monitoring teams) withered away and fell into disuse. Models of change process may help us to explain why this should be the case, but before we move on to this we want you to reflect on the above.

Think about the changes which have occurred in your own organization over the last decade. Try to categorize these changes under the headings of expanded reproduction, evolutionary transition, revolutionary transformation. Which changes have proved the most difficult to implement?

One of the most widely quoted models of change arises from the work of Kurt Lewin. Lewin (1951) argued that change occurs via the three phases of:

— unfreezing
— changing
— refreezing

Unfreezing can be seen as the period during which existing ways of working and values are brought into question. Change refers to the period where new forms of working are introduced. Refreezing can be seen as referring to the consolidation of this new way of working with the establishment of a value system which supports the new state of affairs.

Research (*see* for example Warwick, 1975) on change in the public sector which has used this model suggests that:

- *external factors* (such as the requirements of legislation) are the most important in *unfreezing* the present situation
- *internal factors* (such as training programmes) are the most important in *refreezing* the new situation, and that this is the area which is frequently overlooked (with the consequence that public sector organizations have a remarkable tendency to slip back into former ways of working, so that the change is more apparent than real).

Lewin's model is in fact a little more complex than this. It results from his 'force-field' analysis framework. He argued that organizations exist in a state of equilibrium. This equilibrium (the status quo) is the result of opposing forces (driving and restraining forces) which constantly act upon the organization and its individuals. In order to change the status quo individuals have to identify what change they think is necessary and then identify the driving and restraining forces. The unfreezing process consists of creating an imbalance between the driving and restraining forces. Lewin argued that there is an optimum way of achieving this. First, the restraining forces should be selectively removed, the driving forces should then automatically push change forward. An increase in the number of driving forces, or in the potency of the existing ones, after the restraining forces have been selectively removed should bring about a greater degree of change. This sequencing of action is essential; if the driving forces are strengthened before dealing with the restraining forces the result will be, according to Lewin, an equal and opposite reaction, thus strengthening the restraining forces. We might use Lewin's argument in explaining the strength of the resistance to some of central governments plans. It can be argued that central government have concentrated primarily on strengthening the driving forces (via legislation) and only subsequently when they have encountered greater resistance than expected, have they sought to eliminate some of the restraining forces (or at least opportunities for resistance — e.g. changing teachers contracts with regard to setting and marking tests).

Take one of your own change experiences and try to model it in terms of Lewin's three-stage model of unfreezing, changing, refreezing. What activities were associated with each of these stages?

Research evidence (*see*, for example, Metcalfe and Richards, 1990), particularly prior to the 1980s, suggests that sustained change in the public sector is difficult to achieve. There are a number of reasons why this might be the case.

As we mentioned in the introduction to this book one of the distinguishing features of public sector organizations is their *diffuse pattern of authority*, which makes it difficult for any one individual or group of individuals to have a significant impact on an organization. Kouzes and Mico (1979) argue that public sector organizations consist of people working within three domains: the policy domain (elected politicians), the management domain (managers), and the service domain (the various professions represented in the organization). These three domains may overlap (particularly the management and service domains) but they are frequently in conflict with one another. Each domain has different principles, ways of working and sees success in different terms.

The *resistance to change* offered by *professionals* (such as doctors or teachers) is often singled out in explaining the lack of lasting change in the public sector. This resistance results from individual loyalty to a profession and the objective of that profession to maintain control of its occupation and retain or improve its power in organizational decision-making. Doctors' responses to the *Working for Patients* reforms in the NHS can be seen in this way, as can school teachers' responses to the introduction of national testing. Such resistance appears to be one of the reasons why central government, in recent years, has tried to pave the way for change by an explicit attack on some of the prominent public sector professions (in particular teaching). The resistance to change offered by professionals may also be compounded by inter-professional rivalry.

The *involvement of elected officials* in public sector organizations is often said to lead to short-term horizons and a reluctance to go beyond broad statements of intent into specific details. At the level of specifics some hard choices have to be made and winners and losers are much more clearly identified; hence change proposals might become electoral liabilities. As the oft quoted statement goes:

> It must be considered that there is nothing more difficult to carry out, nor more doubtful of success, nor more dangerous to handle, than to initiate a new order of things. For the reformer has enemies in all those who profit by the old order, and only lukewarm defenders in all those who would profit by the new order, this lukewarmness arising partly from the incredulity of mankind, who do not truly believe in anything new until they have had actual experience of it.
>
> Machiavelli (1513) p. 55.

The sheer *size of many public sector organizations* makes large-scale change difficult. The desirability of equity of treatment and the need for strong accountability mechanisms frequently leads to the establishment of bureaucratic systems and structures which are inherently resistant to change. The nature of bureaucratic organization was considered in Chapter 1; suffice to say here that bureaucratic organizations encourage fragmentation of interests and discourage a concern for what the organization as a whole is doing.

Due to the *need to demonstrate accountability*, change in the public sector is frequently prefaced by wide-ranging consultation with pressure groups, the public at large, service users and professional bodies. This makes the process of introducing change often, necessarily, long-winded. The forms of accountability practised in the public sector also mean that employees are sometimes rewarded for success, but more often are punished for failure. Given that any change involves risk and hence the possibility of failure, there is little incentive to enter into changes willingly.

Metcalfe and Richards (1990) have argued that if change in the public sector is to progress through the three phases of unfreezing, changing and refreezing, then it needs to be sponsored from the top over a prolonged period. As an example of this, Metcalfe and Richards in analyzing change in central government emphasize the important role played by Margaret Thatcher in providing this top level sustained commitment to certain change projects in the Civil Service, such as the Rayner Scrutinies and the Next Steps initiative. However, in highlighting the importance of top level support, it is important not to overplay the importance of politicians or managers. Wilson (1992) points out that the managing change literature tends to assume that managers are all-powerful and hence the role of context (that is, the environment of the organization) is underestimated. The role of context has been shown to be important in understanding change in the private sector. Pettigrew (1985) in analysing long-term change in ICI stresses the importance of changes in the environment. He argues that major change in ICI occurred during times of environmental crises, coupled with a change in leader at the top of the organizations (such as the appointment of Sir John Harvey-Jones). Pettigrew's work on change in the NHS (Pettigrew, Ferlie and McKee, 1992) suggests that the role of context is equally important in understanding change in the public sector.

Another reason why past changes in the public sector have not always lived up to expectations may be the tendency to introduce structural change as a remedy for all ills. Many public sector employees have lived through several structural reorganizations and have become cynical as to what these achieve. The comments often heard are:

— rearranging the deck-chairs on the Titanic
— change for the sake of change
— shuffling the offices.

Changing structures — that is, redesigning the organization in terms of the dimensions of job design, the grouping of jobs/units, rules, lateral linkages and decision-making structures (discussed in Chapter 1) — is only one of the approaches available. Wilson (1992) points out that there are two other approaches to managing change:

- *Cultural approaches* — which focus on the organization climate, ideology and prevailing beliefs
- *Behavioural approaches* — which stress the importance of interpersonal and social psychology in getting individuals to adapt to change.

Attempts to change the culture of public sector organizations appeared to be commonplace during the 1980s following the publication of 'In Search of Excellence'. There is, indeed, a danger that, whereas in the 1970s structural change was seen as the remedy for all ills, in the 1980s and early 1990s cultural change approaches might be adopted as an equally inadequate remedy. As we have already seen in Chapter 1 there is some dispute in any case about whether culture is something which is amenable to managerial manipulation.

Behavioural approaches tend not to have been widely adopted in the public sector. In the latter part of this chapter we consider how some of these approaches may be used to help individuals adapt to change. Whilst behavioural approaches may not have been used as a change strategy, behavioural concepts are often employed when trying to explain failures to bring about change — such failures are frequently blamed on individuals' resistance and inability to adapt.

We have considered a number of reasons why change in the public sector may be particularly difficult to bring about. Consider a change in your own organization which did not work out as was intended. In retrospect why do you think this was so? Were any of the possible reasons we have mentioned so far evident?

Having considered how we can begin to understand the process of change we need now to consider what it all means in terms of how managers should go about planning and managing change. At the level at which you are working you may feel that you have only a limited ability to influence the direction of change and that much of your time is spent implementing and managing the consequences of change decided upon by others. As we stressed in Chapter 3 it is important not to underestimate your ability to influence events and as a last resort you always have the negative power (especially in conjunction with others) of refusing to do something with which you do not agree. You should not see such resistance to change as necessarily a bad thing. What may be rational for one group of people within an organization will not necessarily be rational, or the best plan of action, from the point of view of others.

One of your main concerns is likely to be managing people during times of change, and the latter part of this chapter concentrates upon this. Before moving on to this, however, it is worth spending a little time thinking about the process of planning and introducing change.

Planning and managing change

We should like you to work through this section by considering a change which you may introduce. This may be a change which is being initiated by you or one which you are required to introduce. In the case of the latter it should be in an area where you have some scope for local interpretation.

It is usual to think about the introduction of planned change in terms of the two-stage process of diagnosis and intervention.

- *Diagnosis* refers to understanding why there is a need for change and what sort of change is required. The medical metaphor suggests that in the diagnosis stage you would be observing symptoms and then searching for the causes of these symptoms. Having uncovered the root causes the most appropriate treatment (drawing upon medical science, or in this case organizational theory) would be decided on.
- *Intervention* refers to implementing the treatment in the form of actions to bring about change. These actions may be scheduled to address the three phases of unfreezing, changing and refreezing.

If we use the medical metaphor, then the idea that science always has the answer and that diagnosis and intervention follow one another in two discrete phases can easily be questioned. There are many instances in medicine where intervention (e.g. drugs) is used in a trial-and-error way in order to narrow down the choice of diagnosis. The same can be said of planned organizational change; diagnosis and intervention follow one another in a cyclical pattern

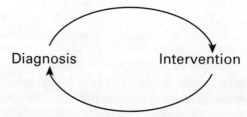

Using your change project make some preliminary notes under the headings of diagnosis and intervention:

- *Diagnosis — what are the problems which you need to address? Why are these problems? What are their root causes? What solutions may be appropriate? Which seem feasible?*

- *Intervention — what actions can you take? Do these need to be staged so that you focus on unfreezing and refreezing as well as changing?*

Much of the mainstream literature on managing change encourages managers to focus on rationally and objectively analyzing the present state of the organization and then appraising the ways in which the organization could change in order to improve its performance. However, the idea that it is possible to diagnose in such an objective manner has to be questioned. We all have favourite ways of seeing things and tend to view any problems from the point of view of our own interests. Managers are encouraged to consult with their workforce and where possible get them to participate in both the diagnosis and intervention stages. Such recommendations tend to underestimate the importance of different interest groups within the organization and the impact of power and politics (remind yourselves of the arguments in Chapter 3). You need to ask yourself who holds power and whose view of what change is needed is dominant. There is a danger of developing a vision of the organization as one happy family, where all share the same interests, with the attendant problem that when members of the 'family' squabble this is seen as dysfunctional. Here we see one of the dilemmas for all managers (be they in the public or private sectors). Much of the prescriptive management literature suggests that they should be rational, objective and consultative, whilst the reality of organizational life involves coalition building, negotiation and bargaining.

Buchanan and Boddy (1992) have considered the role of the change agent and have argued that the myth of rationality and people all pulling together needs to be sustained, but that it needs to be tempered by a more realistic political approach. Change agency, they argue, involves:

1. a *public performance* of rationally considered, logically phased and visibly participative change, and
2. a *backstage activity* of recruiting and maintaining support and seeking out and blocking resistance.

The public performance is what is reflected in written reports, verbal presentations and formal actions. The backstage activity is what takes place behind the scenes in informal discussions and private analyses of the situation. You may, for example, analyze the distribution of power in the organization and which groups are likely to resist change and why. You may then go on to consider how you might persuade those likely to resist the change to agree to it. All of this would be a private analysis and the subject of private discussions. The public performance would underplay the politics and focus on selling the rationale for the change, the consultation process and how the implementation of the change is to be phased.

What public performance is appropriate to your change area? How are you going to sell your change as rational and logical? Whom are you going to involve and how? What backstage activity might you need to undertake to ensure the success of your public performance? How are you going to achieve this in a way which does not undermine the public performance?

Buchanan and Boddy go on to argue that in planning and managing change managers need to have competence (or draw upon the competence of others) in three areas:

- *Technical competence* with respect to the substance of the changes to be implemented. So, for example if the change involves the introduction of a new computerized management information system, then competence in the analysis of such systems is important
- *Planning and monitoring techniques,* such as linear planning and critical path analysis, are important in ensuring that where change 'A' needs to occur before change 'B', this need is identified and scheduled. Monitoring progress should enable plans to be rescheduled and updated as appropriate
- *Process competence* which includes a range of communication, team building, influencing and negotiating skills

The extent to which each of these three areas needs to be emphasized will vary with the change situation. Frequently technical skills and planning and monitoring techniques are prioritized to the detriment of process concerns.

In relation to your own change area, do you have the requisite technical, planning/monitoring and process skills? If you do not have them, how are you going to ensure that these areas are covered?

The literature on managing change abounds with lists of recommendations on how best to address the issues of process. One such list is provided by Schein (1985):

— Present a non-threatening image
— Present arguments in terms of client interests
— Diffuse opposition and bring out conflict
— Align with powerful others
— Bargain and make trade-offs
— Begin as an experiment
— Begin small

Whilst no simple list is going to be applicable in all situations, Schein's recommendations are a useful starting point for managers in many change situations. Where possible, it is argued, it is better to take people with you rather than push them into a change. Stewart (1983) uses the work of the Huthwaite Research Group to distinguish between 'push' and 'pull' styles of introducing change:

PUSH	PULL
Proposing	Seeking information
Giving information	Testing understanding
Shutting out	Building
Works best with power	Works without power
Is high risk	Is low risk
Gets low commitment	Gets high commitment

Is win/lose
Needs enforcement
Is most effective short-term

Is win/win
Self-enforcing
Is most effective in long term

Whilst the 'pull' style seems preferable we should remember (as mentioned earlier) not to fall into the trap of visualizing the organization as if it were capable of being one 'happy family'; change is likely to involve losers as well as winners. Child (1984, pp. 281–2) looks at circumstances in which consultation and participation in implementation are likely to be beneficial:

> It is likely that a participative approach will give its most constructive contribution to the process of change in situations where there is underlying agreement about the objective of the change but where (1) there are differing views about the best way to achieve it and (2) no one party has a monopoly of relevant knowledge or power . . . In a second type situation, however, where there is either total agreement on how to proceed or where management is sufficiently powerful to enforce its preferred solution, participation may well be dismissed as a waste of time. In a third type situation, where there is an inflexible opposition to a proposed change based on fundamental disagreement with the aims of its promoters, consultation and participation are likely to be used simply as opportunities for obstructing implementation.

One way in which managers can begin to decide on an appropriate implementation strategy is, to use Lewin's force field analysis framework (*see* the section on 'Understanding the change process' above) to identify the forces for and against a particular change. Those forces against change can be analyzed using Child's criteria of:

— Is there underlying agreement about the objective of the change?
— Are there differing views about the best way to achieve it?
— Which groups have the most power — does any one group have a monopoly of power?

Using Lewin's framework the change strategy would address the forces against change first, with the answers to the above questions determining how far the strategy will be one of participation or one of negotiation and bargaining. Encouraging and developing the forces for change would be the second element of the strategy.

Work through your change project by following the steps outlined above to:

— *identify the forces for and against change*
— *consider these forces using Child's criteria*
— *outline a strategy for reducing the forces against change and developing the forces for change*

Do the answers to these stages cause you to amend your initial thoughts on an implementation strategy, particularly in relation to whom to involve and how?

The guided reading at the end of this chapter provides further references for those wishing to consider the process of planning and managing change in more detail. For the moment, let us turn to the specific consideration of the effect of change on individuals.

Understanding the effect of change on people

Think back to a fairly recent and relatively major change that occurred within your own organization. What effect did this have upon the people involved?

It is likely that in the above exercise you will have started by thinking about the negative effects of change — demoralization, stress, uncertainty, feelings of being 'at sea', anger, despondency, etc. However, you may also have noticed some positive impacts such as excitement, energy, recognition of new opportunities. Change affects people in different ways, and there are a number of psychological models about what happens to people during times of change. One such model is provided by Carnall (1990) who argues that as people learn to cope with a change they go through five stages (which are very similar to the grieving cycle):

- **Denial** — Denial of the validity of new ideas, but the sense of being a member of a group subject to what is seen as an external threat can lead to increased group cohesiveness
- **Defence** — defending own job and territory. There can be a flurry of activity which has been referred to (Schon, 1971) as dynamic conservatism, which is where people fight hard to stay the same
- **Discarding** — people let go of the past and begin to look to the future. They come to see that the change is both inevitable and/or necessary. Discarding involves letting go and people can feel 'at sea'
- **Adaptation** — trying to make the new system work
- **Internalization** — acceptance and belief. The new way of working becomes the norm

This is not a simple process. People can get stuck and some may never reach the stage of internalization.

Researchers have been concerned to identify the reasons why individuals resist change in the first place. Bedeian (1980) says there are four main reasons for resistance to change:

- Parochial self-interest
    - Threat to core skills and competence
    - Threat to status
    - Threat to power base
- Misunderstanding and lack of trust
    - Lack of information

- Misinformation
- Historical factors
- Low trust organizational climate
- Poor relationships
- Contradictory assessments
  - No perceived benefits
  - An assessment that the proposed change is wrong/ill thought-out
  - Strong peer group norms, which may shape such contradictory assessments
- Low tolerance of change
  - Fear of the unknown
  - Fear of failure
  - Fear of looking stupid
  - Reluctance to experiment
  - Custom-bound
  - Reluctance to let go

The initial resistance can be so strong that individuals never move beyond the stage of defence. Where the reasons for this are low tolerance of change or misunderstanding and lack of trust, managers may be able to help people move through the coping cycle by employing the techniques outlined in the next section. Where resistance and defence are the result of differing interests and contradictory assessments, a behavioural approach to change (which treats individuals as if they were somehow maladapted) is unlikely to be appropriate. In these circumstances the skills of influencing, negotiating and bargaining are required. Such skills were considered in Chapter 3. The remainder of the present chapter considers the behavioural approaches to helping people to cope with change.

Reflect on you own change project: what effect might this have on individuals? Are any of the people affected by the change likely to resist it? If so, what might be the reasons for their resistance?

Helping people cope with change

What does your organization do to help people to cope with change? What do you think they could do?

Organizational change can have a devastating effect on self-esteem and performance. The individuals affected are likely to require help and support to cope with this. Carnall plots the path of self-esteem and performance during the five phases of the coping cycle.

There are a number of things that managers can do to help people move through the coping cycle:

- *Help to rebuild self-esteem* — Given that self-esteem tends to drop during times of change, especially if existing skills and knowledge appear to be devalued, trying to reverse this trend is an important first step. Helping people to understand the details of the change itself may be an important part of rebuilding self-esteem. It will help them in visualizing their own role within the new situation and also reassure them that they have knowledge and skills which will be appropriate. The remaining items in this list are all important as part of helping to rebuild self-esteem. As a manager, a core skill that you will need to assist this process is empathy — seeking to understand the situation from the point of view of others.

- *Provide information* — There is a dilemma here of how much information to provide. Too much and people can be overwhelmed, too little and the rumour machine takes over to fill the information gap. What is 'enough' will need to be decided within the context of each situation. The information which is supplied needs to be intelligible, accurate and timely.
- *Provide training where appropriate* — This is particularly appropriate where people are being asked to exercise new skills. Training is also used as part of the process of trying to inculcate new values and approaches. However, training should not be seen as the instant answer to all problems.
- *Provide scope for experimentation* — People often feel better about a situation when they have been able to experiment with their new role. Pilot projects can help to provide such experimentation, as can secondment, acting up and other staff development schemes.

Figure 12.1: *The coping cycle*

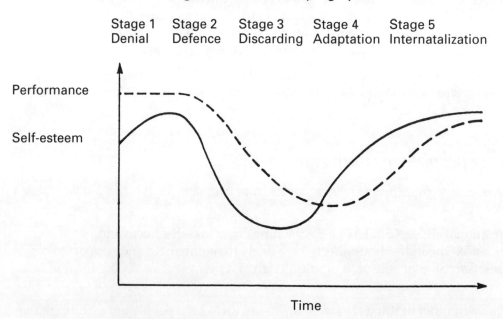

Source: Reproduced from *Managing Change in Organizations* by Carnall, by permission of the publisher, Prentice-Hall International.

- *Tolerate mistakes* — People are unlikely to feel good about experimenting if they know that any mistakes will be noted and may be held against them. Most organizations are not good at tolerating the mistakes which are a natural part of experimentation. We have already pointed out that the accountability practices of public sector organizations are likely to mean that the absence of mistakes is seen as important. As a middle manager you may need to shield individuals from such judgments at a more senior level.
- *Give people time* — Time is often a commodity which is in short supply, but if it is possible to make space by delaying some initiatives whilst pursuing others, then do so. Given that performance tends to drop during times of change, you can also give people time by acknowledging this and ensuring that performance targets are not set too high too soon.
- *Involve people* — We have already discussed the situations in which participation may be desirable. Involvement will sometimes make people feel a part of the change and hence boost their self-esteem. However, if people are involved in too many things then work overload can negate the positive effects of involvement. Also involving everyone at every stage is likely to be too time-consuming and may be construed as a derogation of management.
- *Help to create stability zones* — It is argued that as individuals we can cope with change within certain spheres of our life if we keep other things stable at the same time. Encourage people to maintain these stabilizing anchor points (such as their regular lunch-time stroll) and try not to let work squeeze out all other activities.
- *Provide support mechanisms* — An increasing number of organizations have support mechanisms in the form of mentors, counsellors and formal support groups. These mechanisms are important, but in order for them to be effective there needs to be no stigma attached to their use and confidentiality needs to be respected.
- *Provide appropriate exit doors* — Given that there are likely to be losers as well as winners in most organizational changes, it may be appropriate to provide exit routes for those who lose out. This may mean helping them to think through other job or career opportunities, advising on CV preparation, and writing references. Such exit routes should aim to treat losers in a dignified manner.

Where resistance to change appears to be due to problems of adjustment then an important part of the managerial role is to help people to resolve the issues involved in change and not to do away with opposition in a manipulative way.

Again thinking of your own change project, how will it be appropriate to help people to cope with change? Which of the activities listed above will be appropriate and how might they be achieved?

Conclusions

The management of change is by no means easy or straightforward. There is no magic blueprint for how it should be done. All along the route managers will be faced by a series of dilemmas and choices. Such dilemmas include:

1. participation vs. clear direction
2. gradual change vs. concentration in one major upheaval
3. sharing full information vs. protecting people from uncertainty until decisions are made.

In the public sector change often appears to be forced upon the organization from outside, with little or no consultation. This means that involving people can often only be in terms of how the changes should be implemented and not what the changes should be. This picture may, however, by overly pessimistic and exaggerated. There is usually scope for an organization to impose its own character on a change whilst implementing it, and often only the broad parameters of the change are specified, with many of the details left to local implementation. There are many examples of seemingly imposed changes being renegotiated in terms of both content and timing.

This chapter has sought to enable you to understand better and discuss the process of change. It has considered the stages in the planning and implementation of change and the competences which are required for both of these stages. Finally it has focused on the effect of change on people and how you can help yourself and others cope with change.

Change, as a verb, is ultimately a political activity; change, as a noun, is the outcome of such political activity. We should like to conclude this chapter by making you think about the winners and possible losers in the politics of the changes you have experienced.

Think back over the changes which have occurred during the last five years in your organization: are there any patterns in terms of who are the losers and who are the gainers? Does change tend to marginalize further those groups who suffer differential opportunities, or, on the contrary, does the break with the status quo provide them with opportunities?

References

BEDEIAN, A.G. (1980) *Organization Theory and Analysis*, Dryden Press.

BUCHANAN, D. and BODDY, D. (1992) *The Expertise of the Change Agent: Public Performance and Backstage Activity*, Prentice-Hall.

CARNALL. C. (1990) *Managing Change in Organizations*, Prentice-Hall.

CHILD, J. (1984) *Organization: A guide to problems and practice*, Harper Row.

HANDY, C.B. (1981) *Understanding Organizations*, Penguin Books.

KOUZES, J. and MICO, P. (1979) 'Domain Theory: An Introduction to Organisational Behaviour in Human Service Organizations', *Journal of Applied Behaviourial Science*, **15**, 449–469.

LEWIN, K. (1951) *Field Theory in Social Science*, Harper Row.

MACHIAVELLI, N. (1513) *The Prince*, reprinted by Penguin in 1981.

METCALFE, L. and RICHARDS, S. (1990) *Improving Public Management*, Sage.

PETTIGREW, A. *(1985) The Awakening Giant: Continuity and Change in ICI*, Blackwell.

PETTIGREW, A., FERLIE, E. and MCKEE, L. (1992) *Managing Strategic Change in the NHS*, Blackwell.

SCHEIN, V.E. (1985) 'Organizational Realities: The Politics of Change', *Training and Development Journal*, February, pp. 39–40, quoted in S.P. ROBBINS (1991) *Organizational Behaviour: Concepts, Controversies and Applications*, Prentice-Hall, p. 665.

SCHON, D. (1971) *Beyond the Stable State*, Norton and Co.

STEWART, V. (1983) *Change: the Challenge for Management*, McGraw-Hill.

WARWICK, D. (1975) *A Theory of Public Bureaucracy*, Havard University Press.

WILSON, D.C. (1992) *A Strategy of Change: Concepts and Controversies in the Management of Change*, Routledge.

Guided reading

Two practical guides to planning and managing change are:

PLANT, R. (1987) *Managing Change and Making it Stick*, Fontana.

CARNALL, C. (1990) *Managing Change in Organizsations*, Prentice-Hall.

A very useful book which gets you to think more conceptually about the change process and the pros and cons of some of the quick fix methods is:

WILSON, D.C. (1992) *A Strategy of Change: Concepts and Controversies in the Management of Change*, Routledge.

A good analysis of the role of the change agents, the approaches they can take and the skills which are needed, is provided by:

BUCHANAN, D. and BODDY, D. (1992) *The Expertise of the Change Agent: Public Performance and Backstage Activity*, Prentice-Hall.

If you want to find out more about the politics of the change process, a good starting point would be:

MANGHAM, I. (1979) *The Politics of Organisational Change*, Associated Business Press.

If you want to consider the concept of the 'learning organization' and whether public sector organizations can become more aware, responsive and flexible in the face of changing demands, then a good place to start is:

EDMONSTONE, J. (1990) 'What price the learning organisation in the public sector?', in M. PEDLER, J. BURGOYNE, T. BOYDELL and G. WELSHMAN (1990) *Self Development in Organisations*, McGraw-Hill.

Conclusions: where next?

The intentions of this book were both to help you to develop your understanding of the key concepts and issues facing the contemporary public sector, and to provide you with a range of practical tools with which to enhance your performance as a manager in the public sector. With regard to the former intention, this book has, for example:

- helped you to understand the changing context of the contemporary public sector;
- discussed the key roles and values of the public sector;
- examined the issues involved in developing new services;
- reviewed the issues arising from the changing nature of financial management in the sector.

Similarly, with regard to the latter intention, this book has:

- suggested ways in which you might develop a marketing plan for a unit within your organization;
- talked about how to develop quality management systems;
- offered you a number of strategies through which to manage change in your organization.

These ideas and tools will be immensely useful to you in your role as a manager. However, it would be unrealistic to expect one book alone to meet all your development needs. This would belie the complexity of the tasks which confront you. You therefore need to consider where you go now, with regard to your future development.

A good place to start would be to return to the list of your developmental needs, which you made as part of the Introduction to this book.

Look at this list and consider:

- have you been able to meet all your needs whilst studying this book?
- if not, which ones have you not yet addressed, or addressed only in part?
- has your perception of your needs changed in any way, and if so in what way?
- have you discovered any new developmental needs yourself, which you were not aware of, at the start of this book?

Your answers to these questions will depend upon your own personal and work experience and expectations. Each reader is likely to have a different set of answers. However it would be very suprising indeed if you did not list some unmet needs under at least one of the above headings.

How you choose to meet these needs will vary with your own circumstances. It would be rash indeed for us to suggest one way forward for everyone. However, in this concluding section we list some of the possible ways in which you might tackle your developmental needs in the future. Having reviewed your needs, and considered your options, your next step should be to discuss your future plans with your line manager and your staff development officer.

Avenues for future learning and development

Further reading

Undoubtedly the simplest way forward is further reading by yourself, perhaps guided initially by the suggestions at the end of each of the chapters of this book. This is certainly the cheapest way forward and one that you can pursue at your own pace. The disadvantages are that it may lack any overall coherence and that you will have no one to resort to for advice if you are finding a particular issue or skill difficult to grasp. Nonetheless there are a range of excellent texts available, ranging from the introductory to the advanced, and they offer a relatively cheap accessible source of further learning.

Short courses

Another easily accessible form of training is through short courses. These may be provided either as part of an 'in-house' programme by your organization, or through one of the many external providers of managerial training (these include technical colleges, independent counsultants and professional associations). These are an excellent route to further development, if you have identified a specific skill that you want to develop (such as recruitment techniques or stress management). They may also be the only option available to you from your present employer, because of the cost of other forms of training.

A traditional problem with short courses was that they stood alone and were not integrated with one another, and did not build into recognized qualifications. This problem has, at least in part, been rectified by the development of the system of National Vocational Qualifications (NVQs). These focus upon your ability to demonstrate the possession of the key competencies that are deemed necessary for you to carry out your job. They allow you to build up to recognized qualifications using short courses and they also recognize your prior development (this is known as the Accreditation of Prior Learning, or APL). The NVQ framework is important and may be an advantageous one for you, but it does have two drawbacks. First, it is still developing and does not yet cover all jobs levels and roles. Secondly, it has been criticized by some as allowing employers to provide training on the cheap, rather than upon the basis of identified needs. It is therefore important for you to discover what you can about the NVQ framework for your area of work, and then to discuss the alternatives with your staff development officer.

Advanced practice courses

It may well be that your needs lie in a particular area of practice which faces some very special managerial challenges. If this is the case then you may want to consider a specialist course in this area. These are offered at both further and higher educational establishments. Examples include Master's level courses in the Management of Community Care Services, in Social and Community Development, and in Health Care.

The advantages of such courses are that they will be tailored to your managerial needs as they are now defined. The drawbacks are that, if you do change your organization or role in the future, then you may find that there is limited transferability of these courses to other settings.

Formal management training

The final option, and in many ways the most complete, is to undertake a course of formal management training. This is now available on a full, part-time (usually one day a week), and modular basis, though not all these options are available everywhere in the country. There are also a growing number of courses based upon distance-learning materials. Such courses can lead to the award of:

- Certificates and Diplomas in Management Studies, with the emphasis upon practical skill development;
- Master's (MSc's) and MBAs in Management. These courses concentrate upon understanding the managerial task, as well as equipping you with the skills that you need to carry out the role. They are now available as generic courses in Management and also as specialist courses in such areas as Public Sector Management, Social Services Management, and Health Service Management. For many senior managerial posts in the public sector the possession of such an advanced level qualification is nowadays becoming an essential pre-requisite to appointment.

There are a range of sources for such training, including technical colleges, universities, and also professional institutes. Not suprisingly, this is the most expensive option for your development, though also the one most likely to enhance your career prospects. You may find that your employer will be prepared to second you onto one of these courses, and pay your fees, in return for a promise to return to work for them for a specified period afterwards. A number of professional training organizations (such as the Central Council for the Training and Qualification of Social Workers) also provide bursaries for the fees of recognized courses. Finally you may be able to secure financial support, possibly in the form of an interest-free loan from your local Training and Enterprise Council or from one of a number of independent sources of training support (such as a charitable foundation).

Clearly, undertaking such a course is no light matter and you will need to think through all the implications for yourself. Ultimately, though, it is the one that you may find both most satisfying and most useful in your career development.

The first step will be to get as much information as you can on the courses available in your area (or on distance-learning packages, such as those provided by the Open Business School), and about possible sources of support. Again your staff development officer will be able to help here. There are also lead bodies for training in many areas of the public sector (such as the Local Government Management Board). These can be an excellent source of information and advice.

No one solution is going to be right for everyone. You need to be clear about your needs and choose the option that is right for you. The one thing worse than no training is to find that you have picked the wrong sort for yourself — especially if you are paying for it!

In conclusion, we would emphasize four points:

- do not think of your development as a manager as a 'once and for all' exercise. Your needs will change over time, as will the skills and understanding required for managing in the public sector;
- do use the exercises in this book creatively, with regard to your own job and organization. They are not simply academic exercises, but have been designed to build into your actual work as a manager;
- do be open to new ideas, whatever their source. The rapidly changing nature and context of public sector organizations requires this;
- be clear about your learning and developmental needs for the future, and plan to meet them.

The public sector is an important part of contemporary society, and managing in it is a complex and demanding, but ultimately rewarding task. We hope that our book has helped to enhance your approach to this.